A PADDLER'S GUIDE
to the Rivers of Ontario and Quebec

A PADDLER'S GUIDE
to the Rivers of Ontario and Quebec

KEVIN CALLAN

The BOSTON
MILLS PRESS

A BOSTON MILLS PRESS BOOK

Published by Boston Mills Press, 2003
Copyright © 1999, 2003 Kevin Callan

First printing this edition, 2003

National Library of Canada Cataloguing in Publication
Callan, Kevin
A paddler's guide to the rivers of Ontario and Quebec / Kevin Callan.
Previously published under title: Further up the creek.
Includes bibliographical references.

ISBN 1-55046-387-X

1. Canoes and canoeing—Ontario—Guidebooks. 2. Canoes and canoeing—Quebec (Province)—Guidebooks. 3. Ontario—Guidebooks. 4. Quebec (Province)—Guidebooks. I. Title.

GV776.15.O5C344 2003   797.1'22'09713   C2002-904577-0

Publisher Cataloging-in-Publication Data (U.S.) is available.

Published in 2003 by
BOSTON MILLS PRESS
132 Main Street
Erin, Ontario N0B 1T0
Tel 519-833-2407
Fax 519-833-2195
e-mail books@bostonmillspress.com
www.bostonmillspress.com

IN CANADA:
Distributed by Firefly Books Ltd.
3680 Victoria Park Avenue
Toronto, Ontario, Canada M2H 3K1

IN THE UNITED STATES:
Distributed by Firefly Books (U.S.) Inc.
P.O. Box 1338, Ellicott Station
Buffalo, New York, USA 14205

Cover design by Gillian Stead
Interior design by Mary Firth
Photographs by the author
Maps by Chrismar Mapping Services Inc. Color work by Mary Firth
Printed and bound in Canada by Friesens, Altona, Manitoba

The publisher acknowledges the financial support of the Government of Canada through the Book Publishing Industry Development Program for its publishing efforts.

Contents

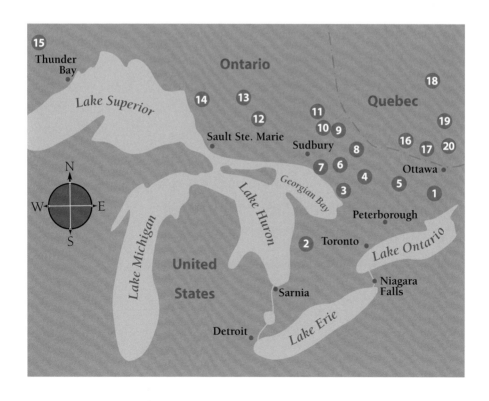

Acknowledgments

WRITING THIS BOOK WOULD HAVE BEEN IMPOSSIBLE without the help of many people. I would first like to thank my canoe companions who tagged along for the fieldwork for this guide: Scott Roberts, Mike Walker, Doug Galloway, Peter Fraser, Scott Bowers, Mark van Stempvoort, Hugh Banks, Mark Robbins, Mike Cullen, Jeff Taylor and brother Greg, Christine Neff, Helen Penny, Len Lockwood, Roy Teer, Rick Wigle, Robin Rivison and his son Glenn, the canoeheads at Boston Mills Press (Noel Hudson, John Denison, James Bosma, Mary Firth, Kathy Fraser and her daughter Mary), my dog, Bailey, and especially my wife, Alana, who's the best canoe partner one could ever ask for.

Special thanks also to Mary Firth, designer extraordinaire (you model a great pair of rainpants, Mary), Kathy Fraser for her editing, and Chrismar Mapping Services for producing all the maps; and to Dan Tyndall of Hikers Haven for being behind me since day one; the gang at Wild Rock Outfitters for their enthusiastic support; the staff at Trent Photographics for their expertise; the friendly staff of the Ontario Ministry of Natural Resources, Canadian Recreational Canoe Association, Ontario Recreational Canoe Association, and the Federation Quebecoise de canot-camping.

Finally, I would like to thank Wally Schaber at Trailhead, Jim Stevens at Eureka, Bill at Ostrom Packs, Peterborough's B & B Outfitting, and the Co-operators Insurance who were all extremely helpful in resupplying me after I was robbed of my gear, not once, but twice during the 1998 paddling season.

Preface

WHY JUST RIVER ROUTES THIS TIME? Well, I always thought when it came to writing down the reason, I would ramble off some poetic philosophy of river travel that I've cherished since boyhood. But when I reminisce about the first time the current's pull proved irresistible, it was actually when a school chum and I floated down the local drainage ditch on slabs of Styrofoam. The incident had nothing to do with any soulful sentiment, a mystery waiting around every bend, or the ache of wilderness solitude that only the journey on a remote river could satisfy. I just wanted to play in the rapids.

In fact, it wasn't until well into my adult life, after paddling a number of rivers and then boasting of them like a Casanova taking inventory of his conquests, that I began truly to understand my love affair with river tripping. There is no better way to feel the ache of wilderness solitude than to journey down a wild river. And if luck has it, you may find a good stretch of whitewater along the way to make things interesting.

Of course, the only way to realize the magic found in moving water is to discover it for yourself. I hope this guidebook encourages you to do just that.

RAPIDS

Class I . . . . . . Easy to moderate
Class II . . . . . . Moderate to difficult
Class III . . . . . Difficult: experience is essential
Class IV . . . . . Extremely difficult
Class V . . . . . . Suicidal

NOTE: Rapids are classed where information was available.

Sam Jakes Inn. A cozy place to spend the night after a day paddling the Rideau Canal.

Decadent Adventure on the Rideau Canal

MOST OF MY TIME SPENT CANOEING IS IN WILD PLACES where muddy portages, bug-infested campsites, and rainy nights spent curled up inside a damp sleeping bag are the norm. Don't get me wrong, I love roughing it out there. But every so often I have this incredible urge to break away from the drudgeries of wilderness tripping and embark on a softer, more comfort-filled adventure — like canoeing on the Rideau Canal.

The Rideau stretches across Eastern Ontario by way of river, lake and channel. Along the way, it passes recreational cottages, elaborate Victorian-style homes, cow pastures and historic villages, each with their quaint bed and breakfasts where hosts serve gourmet meals and offer four-poster beds covered in decorative quilts. This is pure decadence — no dehydrated food, no stuffy nylon tents and, after paying a minimal fee to each lockmaster, no portages.

Construction of the Rideau Canal began in 1826 under Lieutenant Colonel By, who was later relieved of his command for going over budget. The original intent was to help in the defense of Canada against invasion from the United States. The canal provided a safer route than the international boundary along the St. Lawrence for troops and supplies heading out from Montreal toward the settlements of Upper Canada. After its completion in 1832, however, it also played a major role in the Canadian commercial transport system and in the settlement of the Rideau interior. In 1972 the Rideau system was named a Heritage Canal and was placed under the management of Parks Canada, continuing to serve as a navigable waterway.

The center point of this 125-mile (202 km) canal system is Rideau Lake, where the Rideau River flows north and east toward Ottawa and the Cataraquis River flushes south and west into Lake Ontario. Both rivers, now tamed by 23 lockstations and 47 locks, travel through a land of contrasts.

My favorite stretch to canoe lies between Smiths Falls and Beckett's Landing.

This past paddling season, wanting to escape the usual busy summer traffic along the canal, I opted to head out from the town docks at Smiths Falls the first weekend in October. Because the boat traffic is greatly reduced, this time of year is more desirable for canoeists, especially when you can take advantage of the cozy bed and breakfasts along the way.

The Smiths Falls Locks have seen some changes over the years. Concrete has been added to the waste weirs and canal basin, and in 1972 the three combined locks — built to deal with the Rideau River dropping 40 feet in half a mile — were abandoned and a single electric-powered lock was built. But the main locks themselves and the stone arched dam remain unaltered since their original construction.

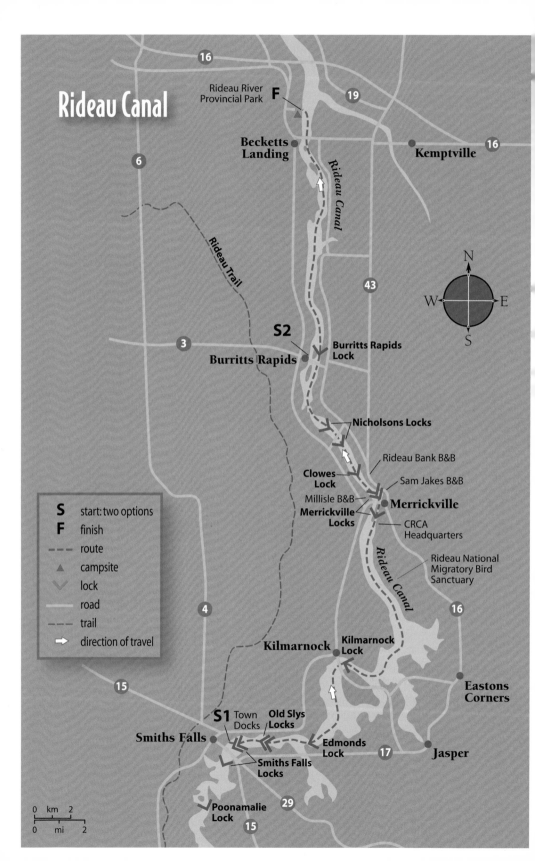

The river channel stays quite narrow until after Old Slys Locks and Edmonds Locks, located almost immediately downstream from Smiths Falls. Once past this stretch, however, the river widens out to a half-mile across.

The shallows here create a broad marsh considered part of one of the most important wetlands in Southern Ontario. Colonel By, along with the thousands of laborers who worked to build the canal, hated muddy areas such as this. Many men became ill with malaria during the canal's construction. However, By's method of building a slackwater canal in land such as this created a perfect habitat for wildlife.

Kilmarnock Lock, originally called Maitland Rapids, is next in line. Following it is another wide stretch of water where there is an extensive marsh and the Rideau National Migratory Bird Sanctuary, known to locals as the Merrickville Wildlife Reserve. You'll want to explore here before continuing downstream to your first layover spot, in Merrickville.

To enter the flight of three locks heading through the town of Merrickville, keep to the long channel on the right that diverts from the main river more than a half-mile (1 km) upstream.

Before you head into town, be sure to pull up on the municipal beach and visit the newly constructed Canadian Recreational Canoeing Association (CRCA) Headquarters. The center has a great assortment of canoe books, videos, maps and periodicals. The CRCA also caters to canoeists traveling along the Rideau system, providing a shuttle service and canoe rental program.

In Merrickville, you'll want to browse through the assortment of craft shops, antique stores, and tea rooms, as well as marvel at the architectural heritage — especially the military blockhouse, a visible reminder of the original intent of the Rideau Canal.

For accommodations in Merrickville, you have a choice of three bed and breakfasts (Sam Jakes Inn, Millisle, Rideau Bank), all conveniently close to the canal. Camping is also available at the Lions Club Campground situated along the south side of the canal, or at the lockstation itself.

From Merrickville the route continues downstream, past well-kept farm pastures, impressive Georgian-style stone houses, and thickly wooded riverbanks. This is my favorite part of the river. You can enjoy a relaxing walk along Nicholson's Locks, near the ghost town map of Andrewsville, before ending the weekend at the small village of Burritt's Rapids, or continue on to Rideau River Provincial Park, over a half-mile (1 km) past Beckett's Landing.

Even though ending at the park makes the last day a long paddle, the section of navigable canal between Burritt's Rapids and Beckett's Landing, titled the Long Reach, is worth the extra effort. The setting of pasture, trees and canal is simply breathtaking — and remember, there's always the warmth of a country inn waiting for you in the next village along the banks of the Rideau.

Rideau National Migratory Bird Sanctuary, considered one of the most important wetlands in Southern Ontario.

TIME 2 to 3 days

DIFFICULTY Only novice paddling experience is needed to travel the Rideau Canal. No Vacancy signs at the inns are likely the only problem you may have to contend with.

PORTAGES Although canoeists can make use of all nine lock-stations, it's important to note that by mid-October the Rideau system shuts down and canoeists must carry around each structure.

BEST TIME TO RUN All season (but after Thanksgiving weekend the locks are closed).

FEE There is a small charge to go through each lock along the canal, and costs are moderate for various bed and breakfasts along the way.

ALTERNATE ROUTE You can make an entire week of it, paddling the canal from Kingston to Ottawa or vice versa.

OUTFITTERS Canoes rentals and shuttle arrangements can be made through the Canadian Recreational Canoe Association, from their new home base in Merrickville.

Canadian Recreational Canoe Association
Box 398
446 Main Street West
Merrickville, Ontario K0G 1N0
613-269-2910
www.paddlingcanada.com

FOR MORE INFORMATION
Friends of the Rideau Canal
1 Jasper Avenue
Smiths Falls, Ontario
K7A 4B5
613-283-5810
info@rideaufriends.com

FOR INFORMATION ON OPERATIONS AND WATER MANAGEMENT
Superintendent, Rideau Canal
34 Beckwith Street South
Smiths Falls, Ontario
K7A 2A8
613-283-5170

Rideau Provincial Park
Ministry of Natural Resources
R.R. 4
Kemptville, Ontario
K0G 1J0
613-258-2740

BED & BREAKFASTS IN MERRICKVILLE
Sam Jakes Inn 613-269-3711
1-800-567-4667
www.samsjakesinn.com
Rideau Bank B&B
613-269-3864 or 1-800-461-3695
Millisle B&B 613-269-3627

MAPS For navigation charts contact the Friends of the Rideau Canal. The Canadian Recreational Canoe Association also has a map of Eastern Ontario canoe routes.

TOPOGRAPHIC MAPS
31 G/4, 31 C/16 & 31 B/13

Bailey's first canoe trip was an adventure, to say the least.

Dog Paddling on the Saugeen

THE SAUGEEN RIVER IS DIFFERENT, I'LL GIVE IT THAT. Threading its way through the farms of Bruce County, it can hardly be thought of as a remote river. But it has a kind of Huck Finn flavor all its own. The nearby hills support cows, corn and old tractor parts. The valley itself, under the watchful eye of the Saugeen Conservation Authority, is home to hundreds of birds and other wild creatures.

Paddling the 65-mile (105 km) stretch of the Saugeen between Hanover and Southhampton was a last-minute decision for me and my wife. We had just become first-time dog owners, and Alana and I thought a short, easy trip would be best to get the dog (a springer spaniel named Bailey) used to canoe tripping. Originally we had planned to paddle a small river in Quebec (Papineau-Labelle's du Sourd River). When we called the park that morning to get directions, however, we were also informed that there was a $3,000 fine for having dogs in the forest reserve. All morning we flipped through maps and guidebooks, and it wasn't until noon that we decided on Ontario's Saugeen River.

The first 13.5-mile (22 km) stretch of river, between Hanover and Walkerton, has the only portages on the Saugeen, making Walkerton seem the better place to put in. Historically, however, the town of Hanover (known back in 1848 as Buck's Crossing) was the original starting point for settlers heading westward. Here they built scows and makeshift rafts and then dismantled them down the river to build the first shanties in the unknown territory called the Queen's Bush. Equipped with a plastic canoe and nylon tent, Alana and I weren't exactly purists when it came to reenacting the past, but we thought it would be neat to at least travel the same route as the pioneers, and pushed off from Hanover rather than Walkerton.

First, however, we had to arrange a shuttle. The normal arrangement made through Thorncrest Outfitters (for the Hanover store call 519-364-5838, and for Southampton call 519-797-1608) is to drive down to their Southampton store on High Street (east off Highway 21), and then continue to the T-intersection and turn left on Carlisle Street, heading to the take-out at Denny's Dam. From there, the outfitter would drive you back up to access the river at Hanover Park. With our late arrival we opted to do the reverse, however. To reach the put-in from the outfitter's Hanover store, we drove west on the main street (Highway 4) and then turned right on 7th Avenue. The municipal park is on the left and we stored our vehicle in the campground parking lot.

The first portage is not far past the Highway 4 bridge. It avoids a concrete dam about 3 yards past a second bridge. The 110-yard (100 m) trail begins to the left of the bridge, crosses the highway to a dirt road, and then follows a path back down to the river.

Numerous shallow swifts and some easy Class I rapids make the Saugeen a perfect trip for first-time river runners.

From the dam the current begins to quicken its pace, with four gravel swifts before Hoffy's Private Campground and several more, including a long Class I rapid, before the first of the two Walkerton dams. There is a 33-yard (30 m) portage to the left of the dam. Alana and I, however, squeezed to the right of a chute and avoided having to get out of the canoe, but I wouldn't suggest this route in high water.

The current continues its fast pace right up until the next Walkerton dam, 1.25 miles (2 km) downstream. Two trails can be used, one to the right (40 yards [35 m]) and the other the left (22 yards [20 m]). At first, Alana and I headed for the take-out to the right. Then suddenly a gun went off in the nearby woods and we quickly ferried ourselves over to use the 22-yard (20 m) trail to the left. It was odd to hear a gun blast so close to town, but as I watched a couple of townspeople walk by and take little notice of the gunfire, I figured it was best to just move on.

After the dam, Alana and I took on some more swifts, passing quickly by a group of fly-fishermen trying their luck for brown trout below the first town bridge, and then a group of teenagers smoking dope under the second.

Just past the second town bridge is a municipal park. We hauled our gear up on the right bank, set it beside a fire grate and a picnic table chained to a tree, and then looked around for a place to pay. All twenty sites were empty, and the only people around to ask for information were the teenagers under the bridge. They were more coherent than I would have thought, and told us to walk across the bridge to Saugeen Country Outfitters and Convenience Store to pick up our camp permit.

We paid the $12 for our night's stay in the park, loaded up with chips and pop, and then headed back to the campground, where now the place was lit up by floodlights from a baseball diamond across the river, and two firetrucks and a police cruiser were parked right across from our campsite. Right away we expected the worst, thinking the dope-smokers under the bridge had vandalized our gear. But it was just Walkerton's volunteer fire department using the park's large field to test their hoses.

It was like being stuck in the Twilight Zone. We went to bed that night to the sounds of spraying fire hoses (they didn't leave until just before 11 p.m.), a junior ball tournament, and the yelps of the Walkerton youth, who had returned to continue their pot party under the bridge. The experience did have its positive side, however. After surviving a night in this modern version of Mayberry, Alana and I figured dealing with all the difficulties of wilderness camping would be a piece of cake.

The Saugeen was alive with birdsong the next morning. The further we paddled away from Walkerton, the wilder the river became. The best set of rapids also happens to be only an hour's paddle downstream from the town. It's here that the Saugeen cuts into the side of the immense Walkerton moraine, exposing a 100-foot-high (30 m) bank of sand and till that has become home to hundreds of bank and rough-winged swallows.

Our dog, Bailey, loved the rapids. Leaning over the bow the entire time, her ears cocked, she lifted her nose to sniff the dampness in the air. It was a perfect place to test her in the canoe. Each channel was well defined and the only real danger was that we might take the wrong route and find ourselves marooned on some gravel bar.

Dealing with the cattle grazing downriver was a different story, however. Bailey went nuts, barking and whining at the timid creatures until they finally had enough of her and retreated back to the barn. It was embarrassing, to say the least, having our dog scare off the local cow population. Surprisingly, however, when it came to sighting any feathered creatures, our bird dog kept completely silent and we managed to build quite a list: a number of turkey vultures perched halfway up a dead elm, a kingfisher around almost every bend, a flock of mergansers that persisted on flying just ahead of us for almost an hour, scads of bobolinks and goldfinches brought in by the nearby fields, three great blue herons, and a rare sighting of a green heron.

In 1879 it took the *Waterwitch* (a flat-bottomed steamer built by David Hanna) only four hours to travel the 24 miles (39 km) between Walkerton and Paisley. It took us eight hours. After traveling through the almost desert-like scenery of overgrazed pastures past McBeath Conservation Area (a campground

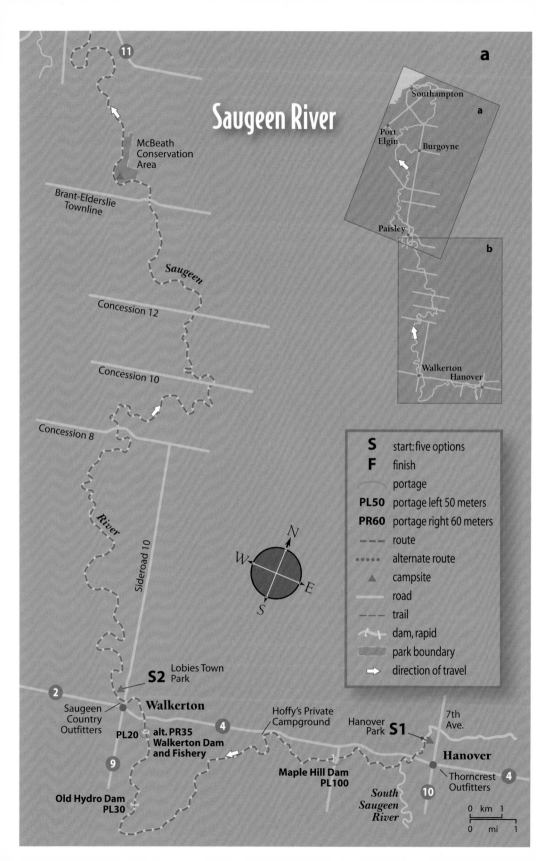

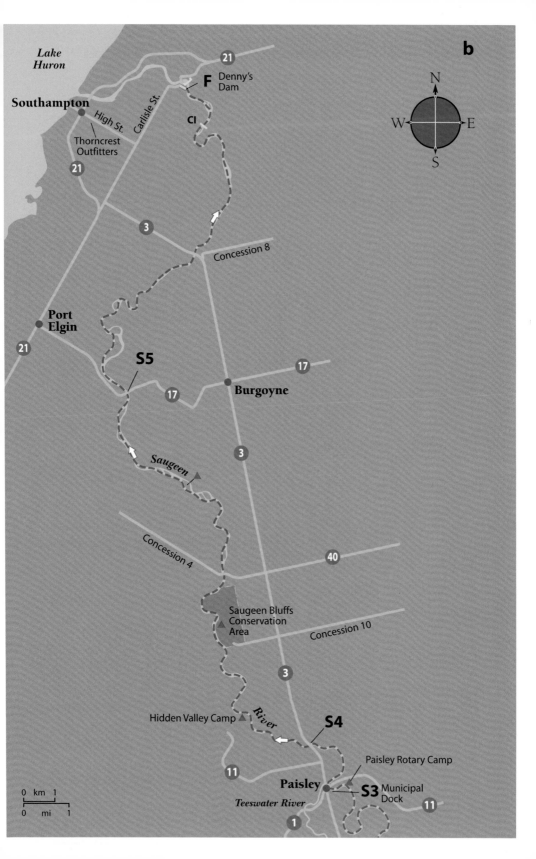

accessible only by water), Alana and I didn't mind our reconnection with civilization at all when we tied up at the municipal dock directly below Paisley's historic fire tower.

There was so much to see and do in this quaint hamlet — browse through shops, visit the local outfitters, and swallow down a pint or two at Libby's Restaurant — that it was well into the afternoon when Alana and I walked back to our canoe and set off downriver to make camp at Saugeen Bluffs Conservation Area.

Shallow swifts sped us along most of the way, especially after Hidden Valley Camp, and by now we had become so proficient at reading the rapids ahead, knowing which channel held the most water and which would scrape the paint off the bottom of our canoe, that we pulled up to the campground on the north shore just a little over an hour out of Paisley.

It would have been cheaper to continue on to some bush site located on one of the Crown land islands another hour downstream. But Alana and I thought it was worth it to splurge on a flush toilet, hot showers, and clean drinking water (personally, I wouldn't even drink filtered water out of the Saugeen). We made use of one of the specially designed canoe campsites at the take-out, right beside the conservation area dock. The staff eventually wandered down to collect their fee.

The next morning we enjoyed bacon and eggs purchased in Paisley the day before, and then set off on the seven-hour paddle to Southampton. The river widens its banks even more here and after the County Road 4 bridge, and especially after the County Road 17 bridge, it splits into definite channels around islands thick with willow and butternut trees. The rapids also continue, parting themselves around boulders, gravel bars, and even the odd car tire and discarded living-room couch. And not far beyond the County Road 3 bridge, where a stunt man from the 1986 movie *One Magic Christmas* plunged a car into the river and didn't come back to retrieve it until a local canoe club sent some angry letters to the Walt Disney Corporation, is an excellent Class I rapid — the most challenging on the river.

Eventually the rapids calm down, around the next bend, and you'll begin to feel the cool wind coming off Lake Huron as you approach the take-out to the left of Denny's Dam.

It is possible to continue your tour of the river by portaging 55 yards (50 m) left of the dam, and then take out at the public boat launch a little way downstream or directly on the public beach in Southhampton. By doing this, you're able to paddle past the historic meeting place where 700 Ojibwa war canoes gathered before heading inland and attacking the invading Iroquois in 1656.

Alana and I were informed by Thorncrest Outfitters, however, that the fast water past Denny's Dam was too dangerous to risk it, and the winds out on Lake Huron can cause problems at times, so we agreed to meet our shuttle driver at the first take-out instead. But somehow we managed to arrive three hours early, and rather than hang around the dam, we decided to ditch our gear in the nearby bushes and take a walk up to the outfitters.

Of course, that was a foolish move. The trip into town took an hour, and by the time we got back to the take-out, all of our gear had been stolen.

Words cannot describe the effect this incident had on us. I was furious. It wasn't just a pile of camping equipment that was taken from us; it was part of our life. The three-season sleeping bag Alana bought me for my birthday, a Therm-a-rest I bought her for Christmas, a compass I received from my father the day I graduated from college, a coffeepot that I had used since high school — all were now sitting in some idiot's car. And, believe it or not, this was the second time I'd been robbed that summer. Just a month before, the door of my truck was pried open with a crowbar while it sat in the parking lot in Algonquin. I was canoeing in the interior at the time, so my gear was safe. But everything else, including my collection of John Denver tapes, was stolen.

Mike, our shuttle driver, couldn't believe what had happened. Thorncrest had always stored their unlocked rental canoes at Denny's Dam and had never had a problem. Even when the police arrived, the officer couldn't understand who could have spotted our stuff hidden in the woods.

At any rate, it was late by the time Mike had us back to our vehicle, which was parked in Hanover, and really late by the time Alana and I got back to Peterborough. But here's the good news. Because we live in the modern age, we have insurance. With the help of the outfitting stores in Peterborough, very good friends, and a cooperative claims adjuster, we were able to put together enough gear to continue our adventures that summer (though we never could find a replacement for that coffeepot). To take away the unpleasant memories of that ill-fated trip, we returned to the Saugeen River. With the late John Denver's "Country Roads" playing on the truck stereo and Bailey now a seasoned paddler, we enjoyed a late fall trip down the Saugeen River.

Dog Paddling on the Saugeen

TIME 2 to 3 days

DIFFICULTY There's an incredible amount of swift water on the Saugeen, but apart from a couple of somewhat challenging Class I rapids, everything can be safely run by novice paddlers.

PORTAGES
3 (none if you put in at Walkerton)

LONGEST PORTAGE
110 yards (100 m)

BEST TIME TO RUN IT The Saugeen is an all-season paddle, but you may have to get out and wade quite a bit if the water level is low.

FEE Apart from the shuttle, each designated campsite is at either at a municipal park, private park, or conservation authority area, where a camping fee is required.

ALTERNATIVE ROUTE Between Hanover and Southampton there are at least nine possible access points to cut your trip short. Some canoeists even venture past Denny's Dam and out into Lake Huron.

OUTFITTERS

Thorncrest Outfitters
193 High Street
Southampton, Ontario
N0H 2L0
519-797-1608
or
309 10th Street
Hanover, Ontario
N4N 1P5
519-364-5838
www.thorncrestoutfitters.com

Cowan Canoes
316 Mill Street
Paisley, Ontario
N0G 2N0
519-353-5535
www.cowancanoes.com

The Greater Saugeen Trading Co.
473 Queen Street
Paisley, Ontario
519-353-4453

FOR MORE INFORMATION

Saugeen River Conservation Authority
R.R. 1
Hanover, Ontario
N4N 3B8
519-364-1255

Ministry of Natural Resources
611 9th Avenue East
Owen Sound, Ontario
N4K 3E4
519-376-3860

Saugeen Country Tourism Association
R.R. 5
Owen Sound, Ontario
N4K 5N7
1-800-265-3127
or 519-371-2071

MAPS The Saugeen Country Tourism Association has produced as pamphlet titled *Saugeen River Canoe Route*. Andrew Armitage's guidebook, *The Sweet Water Explorer: A Paddler's Guide to Grey and Bruce Counties* is also an excellent resource for the river. You can also refer to the Saugeen River map in The Adventure Map series by Chrismar.

TOPOGRAPHIC MAPS
41 A/3 & 41 A/6

Muskoka's Moon River

SINCE THE MOON RIVER IS ONLY TWO HOURS FROM METRO TORONTO, I figured it couldn't possibly compare to some of the more northern trips I've done. But still, while driving north on Muskoka's Highway 69, I would always slow down while passing over the Moon River bridge, take a peek over the guardrail, and wonder what it would be like to spend a weekend paddling down to Georgian Bay.

Then, last spring, I did just that, only to discover that I was right. It wasn't at all like the rivers in the far north. Second-growth forests crowded the banks, a maze of cottages had been built out on the Bay, and hordes of boaters gathered at the river's mouth to swim, fish and generally trash the place. Obviously, it wasn't virgin wilderness. To me, however, it still presented a sense of what was once wild. For canoeists looking for a simple two-day jaunt to recharge their batteries, an adventure on the Moon River is sometimes all that's really needed.

The starting point for the Moon River is on the north side of the Highway 69 bridge and to the left of the roadway. Before heading out, however, arrange to have a second vehicle shuttled to the take-out at the Moon River Marina. To get there, drive north on Highway 69 for 4.5 miles (7 km) and turn left onto Muskoka Road 11. Then, after the town of MacTier (3.75 miles [6 km] in from the highway), take the Healey and Kapikog Lake Road until you pass the entry point for Massasauga Provincial Park (a distance of about 10.5 miles [17 km]), and then another 1.25 miles (2 km) to the marina, where you must pay a moderate fee for parking in their lot before heading back to the river.

Almost immediately past the put-in is a long stretch of rapids called the Seven Sisters. The first rapid comes with no obvious portage, except for a rugged trail on the right, and it must be run or lined down. The second and third, however, are both small chutes, and must be portaged along the rocks to the right. The remaining four are just shallow, rock-strewn rapids, not too severe but all of them exciting — as long as the water levels stay up. If levels are low, you'll have to wade or line down most of them.

Next, after a 2-mile (3 km) calm stretch, is Curtain Chute. This is place where the bodies of two drowned canoeists — Jack Kim and Bong Sung Lee — were recovered during the spring of 1997. Their deaths attest to the severity of the rapids and the importance of the 242-yard (220 m) portage that runs along the top of the rock ledge to the left. The accident occurred during a spring outing at, surprisingly, 2:30 a.m. According to police reports, one of the seats in their ten-year-old, 14-foot fiberglass canoe gave way and caused it to tip over. Considering the temperature of the water was not much above freezing, and neither of the two men was wearing a lifejacket, they didn't stand much of a chance.

Downstream from Curtain Chute, after the river narrows and then bulges, spreading out around a flattened island carpeted in swamp maple, Twin Rapids comes into view. Here, the river is divided into two main channels by a large island of rock and pine. You will first spot the right channel, a rock-studded chute with a 197-yard (180 m) portage on the right and prime campsites on either side of the drop. The left channel is just around the corner. It has a much more vertical drop to it, making an extremely steep and hazardous put-in for the 131-yard (120 m) portage on the right, which also happens to be covered in poison ivy.

Both channels can be taken. Note, however, that both end with a set of rapids. The left has a small chute that can easily be portaged 55 yards (50 m) on the left or, in low water, can be simply lifted over on the right. The right channel is a different story, though. It has a much sharper drop with no direct way to walk around it except for a rugged bush trail on the left.

The Moon River converges at the end of the two channels. Around the corner to the left is Moon Falls. The cascade drops twice before flushing out into the waters of Georgian Bay. You can either take on the full 490-yard (450 m) portage on the right or shorten your walk by paddling the elongated pool in between.

Possible campsites are all around this spot. However, even though the tumbling cascade makes for a dramatic place to spend the night, I strongly recommend you set up camp upriver, either above or below Twin Rapids. Here

Moon Falls.

Alana dishes out shrimp alfredo at the Twin Falls campsite.

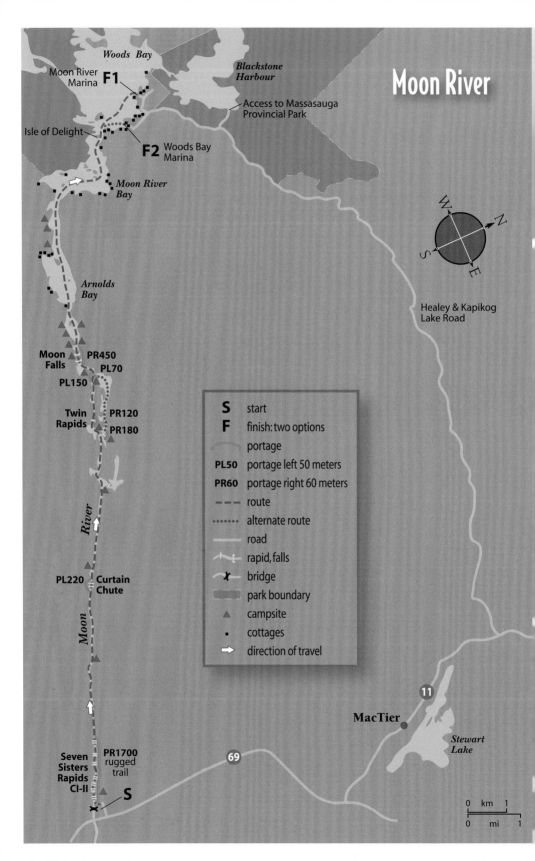

you won't be bothered by the crowds of cottagers gathering for a day's outing. As well, the network of rock ledges, tumbled boulders, and fallen cedars hanging low over the bank make for excellent bass-fishing an hour before dusk.

From Moon Falls it's a simple case of navigating through the maze of rocky islands scattered throughout Arnolds Bay, Moon River Bay, and finally, Woods Bay. And as long as you keep close to the right-hand shoreline, especially after passing Isle of Delight, you'll find it easy to locate the docks of Moon River Marina. Be warned, however, that you'll have to make an early-morning paddle here — not only to avoid the brisk winds that quickly make paddling unbearable, but also to get off the water before the local Sea-doo population begins to swarm around you.

Muskoka's Moon River

TIME 2 days

PORTAGES 6

LONGEST PORTAGE
490 yards (450 m)

DIFFICULTY The Moon's Seven Sister Rapids are dangerous during high water, but after early spring the river calms down and is perfect for the novice.

BEST TIME TO RUN IT
Late spring and early fall.

FEE The route travels through Crown land, where no fee is required for Canadian citizens. However, a fee is charged to park your vehicle at the Moon River Marina.

ALTERNATIVE ROUTE You can avoid shuttling a vehicle and navigating down Seven Sisters Rapids by paddling upstream from Woods Bay to Twin Rapids and then returning via the same route.

OUTFITTERS
Swift Canoe & Kayak (Georgian Bay)
Highway 400 North
Box 604, Waubaushene, Ontario
1-800-661-1429
georgianbay@swiftcanoe.com

White Squall Wilderness Shop
R.R. 1
Nobel, Ontario
P0G 1G0
705-342-5324
or
19 James Street
Parry Sound, Ontario
P2A 1T4
705-746-4936
www.whitesquall.com

FOR MORE INFORMATION
Ministry of Natural Resources
Parry Sound District Office
7 Bay Street
Parry Sound, Ontario
P2A 1S4
705-746-4201

TOPOGRAPHIC MAP 31 E/4

Taking it easy on Algonquin's Oxtongue River.

Algonquin's Oxtongue River

LOOKING THROUGH THE HISTORY BOOKS, you might come to believe that everyone who has ever visited Algonquin, before and even after the provincial park was formed, first paddled into the region by way of the Oxtongue River. Lieutenant Henry Briscoe became the first-recorded white person to travel the Oxtongue in 1826 while searching for a secure military route between Lake Huron and the Ottawa River. (The project was abandoned due to the river's numerous falls and rapids). Alexander Shirreff attempted to promote settlement in the region during a trip in 1829; David Thompson mapped the waterway in 1837. He was followed in 1853 by Alexander Murray, the first chief ranger of Algonquin, who traveled up to Canoe Lake in 1893 to construct the first park headquarters. Well-known artist Tom Thomson camped along the Oxtongue when he first visited the park in 1912.

More recently, however, you'd be hard-pressed to spot many other canoeists traveling the river. I'm not sure why. It could be because of its close proximity to busy Highway 60 (traffic can be heard along some sections) or maybe because canoeists believe the park has more to offer elsewhere. Whatever the reason, however, I find it one of the most rewarding weekend jaunts Algonquin has to offer — so much so, I even wonder why the heck I'm telling you about it.

There are various places to begin your trip down the Oxtongue, but the Canoe Lake access point seems to be the overall favorite. First, however, a second vehicle must be dropped off at the preferred take-out point — Algonquin Outfitters (705-635-2243) — which is located on Oxtongue Lake, just west of the Highway 60 bridge. After making arrangements to leave your car at the outfitters' parking lot, head back out to the highway and drive east toward the park (Algonquin Outfitters may provide a shuttle). The road leading off Highway 60 to the Canoe Lake access point is marked to the left, 9.5 miles (14 km) past the West Gate. You can either put in at the beach site or at the docks beside the Portage Store.

Not far out on Canoe Lake, the route heads southwest across Bonita Lake and Tea Lake. Don't be fooled by the crowds here. Daytrippers from Canoe Lake and campers from Camp Tamakwa (founded in 1937 by Lou H. Handler of Detroit) and the Tea Lake Campground (an alternative access point) can make canoe traffic a bit hectic at times. Once you get to the far end of Tea Lake and take the 262-yard (240 m) portage marked to the right of Tea Lake Dam, however, the crowds quickly disappear.

Tea Lake Dam was where artist Tom Thomson made camp while on his first visit to Algonquin. The trip was to be a warmup to his two-month expedition down the Mississagi River (see the Mississagi River chapter for details). He later returned to Tea Lake Dam in 1914 to paint, and even guided fellow artist A. Y. Jackson to the very same spot.

You'll encounter only a couple of small swifts on the river before reaching another historic stop — Whiskey Rapids. Here, sometime near the turn of the century, two log-drivers lost a three-gallon keg of whiskey. They were appointed by their fellow workers to head up the Oxtongue to pick up the precious cargo at the Canoe Lake Railway Station. Everything was going as planned, that is, until they decided to stop for a drink or two on their return trip. It was dark by the time they reached the rapid, and, having spotted the take-out for the portage at the last minute, the drunkards chose to run down the whitewater while it was in spring flood. They made it but the barrel of whiskey was never found.

The present-day portage around Whiskey Rapids is an easy 209 yards (190 m) and is marked to the right. Just be sure to keep to the left when the trail forks halfway along.

Downstream, not far past another shallow rapid that can be either run or waded down, depending on water levels, the waterway begins to meander all over. This calm stretch of river, winding its way around pine-clad bluffs on one side and spilling quietly past islands covered in alder and dogwood on the other, is a great place to spot a moose, especially in early spring when almost every salt-deprived moose in the park is attracted to the road salt left along the highway close by.

It will take about an hour's paddle from Whiskey Rapids before the footbridge for the Western Uplands Hiking Trail comes into view. This is another possible access point for canoeists looking for a much shorter weekend on the Oxtongue. And from there, it's another hour's paddle before the river picks up speed again, first at a series of insignificant swifts and then, shortly after, at the more noteworthy Upper and Lower Twin Falls and Split Rock Rapids. Both cascades have short portages (262 yards and 110 yards [240 m, 100 m], each marked to the left). However, the take-out for Split Rock Rapids is incredibly steep and is uncomfortably close to the edge of the falls, especially during high-water levels. So you may want to play it safe and head for shore a few yards further upstream to make use of an extended bush trail.

The river continues to meander for another three hours, passing by what Alexander Sheriff perfectly described in his 1829 journal as "A level, sandy valley, timbered chiefly with balsam, tamarac, and poplar, beyond which, however, the hardwood rising grounds are seen seldom a mile distant on either side." Then, not far past where Algonquin Provincial Park ends and Oxtongue River/Ragged Falls Provincial Park begins (the border is marked by a small creek on the left that leads to the nearby highway), the river drops down five sets of shallow rapids before plunging over the 33-foot-high (10 m) Gravel Falls.

All five rapids can be run. The first and fourth each have a portage (55 yards and 88 yards [50 m, 80 m]) marked on the left just in case. You may

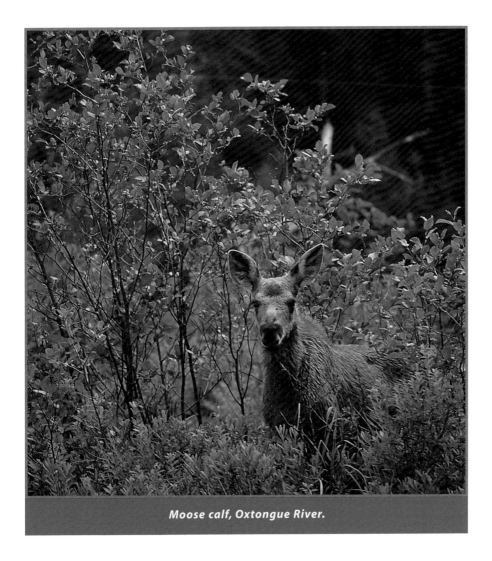

Moose calf, Oxtongue River.

also want to wade down the fifth set, which is only a few yards above the brink of the falls.

Gravel Falls comes with a long, 1,100-yard (1,000 m) portage, marked to the right. Don't worry — experienced whitewater paddlers can put in directly below the falls (reducing the portage to 220 yards [200 m]), and even we mere mortals have to carry only about halfway and then can run the swift water that remains.

The current continues its fast pace all the way to Ragged Falls, located about another half hour downriver. This is an even more scenic cascade than Gravel Falls — dropping three times its height — but it's also a day-use area, and I find the trip quickly loses its wilderness appeal the moment you run into the crowds of tourists who walk in from the highway. As well, the network of trails leading

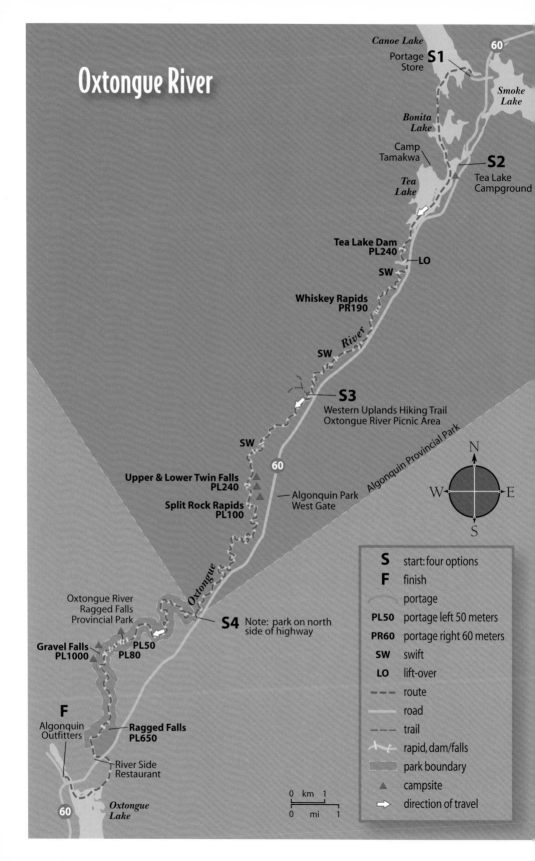

Oxtongue River

Canoe Lake

Portage Store **S1**

60

Smoke Lake

Bonita Lake

Camp Tamakwa

S2
Tea Lake Campground

Tea Lake

Tea Lake Dam
PL240

— **LO**

SW

Whiskey Rapids
PR190

SW River

S3
Western Uplands Hiking Trail
Oxtongue River Picnic Area

SW

60

Upper & Lower Twin Falls
PL240

Split Rock Rapids
PL100

— Algonquin Park West Gate

Algonquin Provincial Park

Oxtongue River
Ragged Falls
Provincial Park

Oxtongue

S4 Note: park on north side of highway

Gravel Falls
PL1000   **PL50**
PL80

F

Algonquin Outfitters

Ragged Falls
PL650

River Side Restaurant

60   **Oxtongue Lake**

S	start: four options
F	finish
⌒	portage
PL50	portage left 50 meters
PR60	portage right 60 meters
SW	swift
LO	lift-over
- - -	route
——	road
- - -	trail
⋏⋏	rapid, dam/falls
▧	park boundary
▲	campsite
⇨	direction of travel

N
W — E
S

0   km   1
0   mi   1

back and forth from the falls make finding the exact whereabouts of the portage (710 yards [650 m] and marked to the left) extremely frustrating. There are, however, small florescent squares on the trees to help point you in the right direction.

From Ragged Falls it's an easy paddle to the Highway 60 bridge, where you can pull into the unique River Side Restaurant for coffee and cake. From here, you simply continue for another twenty minutes, out into the expanse of Oxtongue Lake. By keeping to the right-hand shore, you'll eventually paddle under the Highway 60 bridge again, and then take out at the familiar Algonquin Outfitters to your left.

Algonquin's Oxtongue River

TIME 2 days

PORTAGES 11

LONGEST PORTAGE
1,100 yards (1,000 m) (can be easily reduced to 220 yards [200 m] by running some rapids below Gravel Falls)

BEST TIME TO RUN IT
Spring through fall

FEE The upper section of the river is in Algonquin Provincial Park, where an interior camping permit is required, as well as a parking permit for the Canoe Lake and Western Uplands Hiking Trail access points. However, the lower section is in the Oxtongue/Ragged Falls Provincial Park, where no permits are required.

ALTERNATIVE ROUTE There are great number of alternative access points along the river, allowing for various daytrip possibilities.

OUTFITTERS
Algonquin Outfitters
  (Swift Canoe Co.)
R.R. 1, Hwy. 60
Dwight, Ontario
P0A 1H0
705-635-2243
www.algonquinoutfitters.com
Portage Store
Box 10009
Huntsville, Ontario
P1H 2H4
705-633-5622
www.portagestore.com

FOR MORE INFORMATION
Algonquin Provincial Park
Ministry of Natural Resources
Box 219
Whitney, Ontario
K0J 2M0
705-633-5572 (information)
1-888-668-7275 (reservations)

MAP You can also refer to the Oxtongue River map in The Adventure Map series by Chrismar.

TOPOGRAPHIC MAPS
31 E/7 & 31 E/10

The Little Bonnechere

THE MADAWASKA HIGHLANDS OFFERS WHITEWATER ENTHUSIASTS a great assortment of technical rivers. But for the novice, runs such as Snake Rapids on the Lower Madawaska and Roller Coaster Rapids on the Opeongo River can be a little overwhelming. That's why I like the Bonnechere. I'm not talking about the almost unnavigable stretch of the river that flows through Algonquin Provincial Park, a place Jim Fraser, the Superintendent of Bonnechere Waterway Park, calls "an odyssey, not an adventure." I'm talking about the much easier section between Algonquin's Basin Depot and Round Lake. It's a perfect weekend destination for family vacationers or for canoeists who can't help but cringe at the idea of being pounded down boiling whitewater like laundry in the rinse cycle.

There are a number of spots from which you can access the river, but the main starting point is at Algonquin's Basin Depot — a past supply and stopping site for loggers working for Barnet and McLachin Companies between 1850 and 1913. From Highway 62, turn onto Turner's Point Road, 4.5 miles (7.3 km) north of Round Lake Center. It's 10 miles (16 km) to the park boundary and six more to Basin Depot. But before heading up Turner's Point Road, you should drop a second vehicle off at either Bonnechere Provincial Park or the outfitters at Round Lake Variety, just over half a mile (1 km) south of the park. Parking permits for Algonquin's Basin Depot can also be picked up at Turner's Camp, 3 miles (4.8 km) along Turner's Point Road, which is an alternative take-out.

Be sure to take a walk among the ruins of Basin Depot before you head out on the river. In its prime, the depot supplied up to ten McLachlin Brothers' shanties, offered a stage from the railway at Cobden for $2. Mail arrived at the post office once a week. By 1886 the stage fare had risen to $3 and the extended community supported more than fifty people. Only one of the ten original buildings remains intact. This well-constructed log home was built by the McLachlin Lumber Company in 1892 (making it the oldest standing building in Algonquin) and served as a hospital during a diphtheria epidemic and as a school from 1911 to 1913. At least seven grave sites remain as signs of the outbreak. The markers, hidden in a grove of poplar trees behind a farm shed, are almost impossible to find, however, and your time is better spent searching for the graves of two log drivers who were buried alongside the south bank of Basin Creek.

After your tour of the site you can access the river by following the rough road heading toward the river through a clearing. Park your vehicle near the slab of cement that marks more remains of the two farm sites in the area, and

Silver maple hangs low over the muddy meandering banks of the upper section of the Bonnechere.

continue down to the Bonnechere by walking a narrow path overgrown with grass and raspberry cane.

A quick glance at the river from here will tell you what the trip down to Couchain Lake will be like. If the tea-colored water is flowing easily over the cobblestone, then you're in luck. If not, there's likely not enough water to easily navigate the upper section, and I suggest you don't even bother with it. Instead, drive back along Turner's Point Road and make use of the Couchain Lake access point, 1 mile (1.7 km) past the park boundary. (No park permit is required to park here.)

So why even bother with the two-and-a-half hour paddle on the upper section? Well, I think it's the best part of the Bonnechere. At first the river passes through a typical northern landscape of pine and sand. But after the halfway point, where two portages (a 120-yard [110 m] to the left and a 572-yard [520 m] to the right) avoid a double set of shallow and easily run rapids, the atmosphere quickly changes. Silver maple appears, hanging low over muddy,

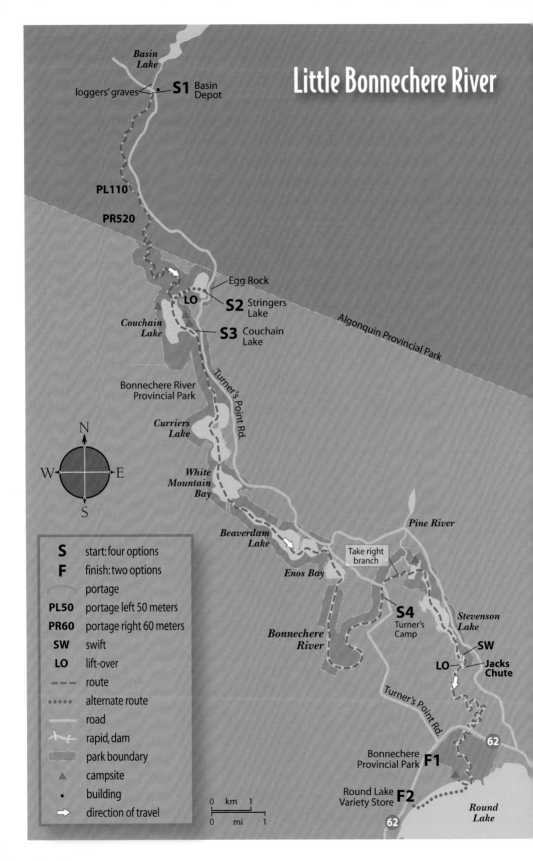

Little Bonnechere River

Basin Lake

loggers' graves

S1 Basin Depot

PL110

PR520

Egg Rock

LO

S2 Stringers Lake

S3 Couchain Lake

Couchain Lake

Algonquin Provincial Park

Bonnechere River Provincial Park

Turner's Point Rd.

Curriers Lake

White Mountain Bay

Pine River

Beaverdam Lake

Take right branch

Enos Bay

S4 Turner's Camp

Stevenson Lake

SW

LO **Jacks Chute**

Bonnechere River

Turner's Point Rd.

62

Bonnechere Provincial Park

F1

Round Lake Variety Store **F2**

Round Lake

62

S	start: four options
F	finish: two options
⌒	portage
PL50	portage left 50 meters
PR60	portage right 60 meters
SW	swift
LO	lift-over
– – –	route
•••••	alternate route
——	road
�	rapid, dam
▮	park boundary
▲	campsite
▪	building
➔	direction of travel

N
W E
S

0   km   1
0   mi   1

Basin Depot, the oldest standing building in Algonquin Park.

meandering banks, making the river almost savannah-like. Belted kingfishers swoop down across the river. The pileated woodpecker's hysterical call echoes throughout the back woods. And around almost every bend, you could catch sight of white-tail deer.

An hour through this lowland swamp, give or take a few necessary lift-overs, and the pine forests return. The river empties out into Couchain Lake. There, three of the four campsites en route are marked and maintained by Bonnechere Provincial Park staff. The two largest sites are found on the southeast end of the lake, just before where the waterway narrows; the other site is off on its own on the northwest side, overlooking the scenic bluff called Egg Rock.

Beyond Couchain Lake is easy paddling across Curriers Lake, White Mountain Bay (named for the steep rock wall to your right), Beaverdam Lake and Enos Bay. Then the river narrows again, twisting and turning its way toward Turner's Camp and Turner's Road bridge. Once past the bridge the river forks. Go right here (the left channel is much shallower) and paddle out into Stevenson Lake.

The fourth designated campsite is marked on the top end of Stevenson, just past where the Pine River empties into the Bonnechere. Depending on how leisurely your paddle was so far, you may want to either make camp here for one final night or continue on downstream to Bonnechere Provincial Park on Round Lake. There's not much to contend with directly after Stevenson Lake, only two shallow swifts and a small drop called Jack's Chute. The swifts can be run, lined or waded down. Jack's Chute can be run — by experts — or lifted over on either side. Just keep in mind that the land alongside Jack's Chute is private and should be respected.

A major problem, however, does occur further downstream, where the river continuously winds back on itself. In 1861, surveyor Robert Hamilton made note of this "exceedingly torturous" stretch of river. He avoided the oxbow by making use of a long portage built by the settlers of the area. Present-day canoeists, however, will find that the old portage no longer exists. The only way to deal with the problem is to grin and bear the monotonous paddle and hope that the fry-truck outside the park gate is open for business when you're done.

The Little Bonnechere

TIME 2 days

DIFFICULTY Perfect for novice canoeists.

PORTAGES 3 (may not be necessary)

LONGEST PORTAGE
572 yards (520 m)

BEST TIME TO RUN IT
Spring through fall

FEE An interior camping permit (sold by Turner's Camp on Turner's Point Road) for Algonquin Provincial Park is required only if you plan to start out from Basin Depot.

OUTFITTERS
Round Lake Variety
R.R. 5, Box 21
Killaloe, Ontario
K0J 2A0
613-757-2162

FOR MORE INFORMATION
Bonnechere Provincial Park
Box 220
Pembroke, Ontario
K8A 6X4
613-757-2103
1-888-668-7275 (reservations)

MAP You can also refer to the Bonnechere River map in The Adventure Map series by Chrismar.

TOPOGRAPHIC MAP 31 F/12

The Restoule–Upper French Loop

THE IDEA TO PADDLE the Restoule–Upper French River system was initiated at a gathering of my regular canoe companions one cold winter night. It seemed that after five continuous trips to Algonquin's interior, a change of scenery was in order. We all sat around my kitchen table and spent a good part of the evening looking over an assortment of maps and guidebooks, trying desperately to come to a group consensus. It was just before midnight when we all agreed upon these two rivers west of Lake Nipissing. Some said they were keen on fishing some of the remote stretches for pike and walleye; others liked the idea of the route forming a loop, saving us the hassles of organizing a lengthy car shuttle; the remainder agreed simply because they were getting tired of looking over maps and wanted to head off for bed.

As it turned out, the Restoule–Upper French River system ended up being one of our favorite routes. We highly recommend it to all those other Algonquin regulars looking for a change of pace.

To reach the starting point, take Highway 11 to the town of Powassan. Then turn left onto Highway 534 and follow the signs for Restoule Provincial Park. When you reach the park, rather than enter through the gatehouse, take the dirt road just to the right and make use of the free parking at the Stormy (Patterson) Lake access point.

From the government dock the route heads west, across Stormy Lake and toward the Restoule River. Eventually the banks close in and you'll have to take the 295-yard (270 m) portage marked to the right of Scott's Dam.

Lennon Lake is next — more a widening in the river than an actual lake — and is soon followed by another 295-yard (270 m) portage, this time marked to the right of MacArthur's Rapids — a technical Class II.

I remember this portage well. It had been raining hard since our group left the parking lot and we welcomed the chance to bail out our canoes and pile on more layers for warmth beneath our raingear. The foul weather had left some of us feeling hypothermic. At the end of the portage the group agreed to huddle under a tarp and contemplate our next move. Some of us were about ready to call it quits and retreat back to the vehicles. Others had the insane idea of breaking into a nearby cabin. My partner, Scott, had a totally different plan. He urged us on, even suggesting that we carry the canoes back up the portage to run the rapids.

We were slow to agree. It's not that we expected good weather; we had all come to grasp the realities of heading out so early in the season. But this year, conditions seemed harsher than reasonable; spring was already two weeks behind schedule and the constant rain was making the river level rise to a record high. But it eventually occurred to us that almost every trip of ours has begun in the rain. So, except for running MacArthur's Rapids, we took Scott's advice and continued on our way.

Three-and-a-half miles (5.5 km) downstream from MacArthur's Rapids you'll come to a bridge. Our maps showed a steep gorge here, but it's not until the river twists its way northward and then over a small chute (use the lift-over to the right) that the Restoule River actually plunges down toward the French. Take note, however, that once you've made it past the chute, you have to make sure to keep to the extreme right until you spot the portage marked on the north side of the river. Scott and I, not knowing how close the drop actually was, followed along the left bank and were almost flushed through the gorge when we blindly nosed our canoe around the bend.

The falls create spectacular scenery but dangerous portaging. The 800-yard (730 m) trail comes with a confusing network of side trails and ends with an abrupt rocky slope.

One could consider camping here — two campsites are located alongside the trail — but our group was looking forward to stopping on one of the small island sites out on the French River. So we continued on, paddling west out of Restoule Bay and then east, up the French River, keeping between the main shore and Boom Island. The further we went, however, the more swollen the river became. Every island campsite was completely flooded over and we had to resort to pitching our tents on a mound of rock beside Leonard Portage — a 60-yard (55 m) trail that leads across the peninsula east of Keso Point, used to avoid Cradle Rapids during high water.

We were all beyond cold by this point and desperate for a fire. There was no dry wood to be found anywhere, but Peter the Pyro saturated a ball of toilet paper in stove fuel and quickly ignited some wet timber. Of course, we all began to lecture him on the dangers of using gas as a firestarter — at least, that is, until the flames started giving off heat. Then we gathered around to soak up the warmth.

By morning the rain had finally stopped. We crawled out of our damp cocoons to discover that the river had risen enough to reduce Leonard Portage to a mere lift-over. But the sun was out, so we all took time to hang our gear out to dry before breaking camp.

From the put-in of Leonard Portage the river splits in two directions; to the left is the Lower and Upper Chaudiere Rapids and to the right is the historic Portage Channel. As far back as the 1880s, plans were set to build an enormous ship canal through here, linking Montreal and Georgian Bay. The ambitious project was soon abandoned but the control dams were still built, Chaudiere Dam between 1910 and 1916 and the Portage Dam from 1949 to 1950. The structures were meant to keep water levels stable on Lake Nipissing and provide a measure of flood control.

Our group chose the Portage Channel, making use of the Chaudiere Portage to navigate around the Portage Dam. This was once the choice route for Natives, fur traders, explorers and missionaries as they traveled the continental

Our group takes advantage of a rare calm spell out on Lake Nipissing.

east-west canoe route. The existing 660-yard (600 m) portage, marked on the south shore, is not the exact trail used, however. The construction of the spill-way flooded a considerable portion of the original portage.

The modern portage first crosses the road heading over to Okikendawt Island and Dokis Village, the central part of the Dokis Indian Reserve. Once past the road, the path heads up and over a steep rise and then through a low-lying area that was completely flooded over because of spring rains. By then, however, our group had learned to adapt to the changing river environment, and we jumped in our canoes and paddled across the soggy portage.

What remains upstream from here is not exactly wild. Logging, farming and, more recently, tourism have changed the landscape. But I still find it intriguing to paddle past such places as Casa Blanca Lodge, Drunken Island and Dokis Village. And the campsites, especially the ones situated on the south-eastern tip of Summer Island (at the mouth of Satchel's Bay), are far enough away from the business of the main channel. We chose to spend our second night here, ending the day early so as to take more time out to dry our gear soaked by the day before's downpour. Peter lit a fire, this time without the aid of gasoline, and we dangled our assortment of clothing over the flames to speed up the drying process. The hot flames did more harm than good, however. Scott burned a pair of wool socks and I somehow managed to scorch my underpants.

The next morning was the opening of the fishing season. We were all up before dawn, setting up our fiberglass rods and snapping on our favorite lures. An hour of casting, however, produced nothing. I was disappointed, to say the least. My father took me fishing on the Upper French when I was a boy, and this same area had always provided plenty of fish.

The author forcing a smile for the camera while slogging through yet another wet portage.

I'll never forget one trip in particular. We were staying at a nearby lodge, sharing a cabin with two off-duty detectives from Detroit. All week these two Americans had trolled for muskie unsuccessfully. Then, on the eve of their last day, the detectives went out for one last try. An hour later my father and I heard a loud bang! Believe it or not, the two fishermen landed a monster fish and then subdued it with their revolver, leaving a large bullethole in the bottom of their boat. By stuffing a jacket into the opening they were able to control the leak long enough to make it back to shore.

We obviously wouldn't have any need for firearms, let alone a landing net, on our group's trip. By the time we traveled upriver to the entrance of Lake Nipissing we had caught only one small pike — about the same size of the lure it was hooked on. We were luckier with the weather, however. It was a morning of calm — no wind, easy paddling, mild sun — and the short trip out to Frank's Bay, which can be dangerous on a windy day, was pleasantly uneventful.

At the southwestern end of Frank's Bay is the entrance to Shoal (Bass) Creek, where the route heads south, back toward Stormy Lake (which is also called Patterson Lake). The three portages en route (99 yards, 60 yards and 50 yards [90 m, 55 m, 45 m], all marked to the left) are easy carries. But the upstream paddle on the creek itself can be quite a challenge. In midsummer, countless beaver dams and uprooted trees can make the way completely unnavigable. During a spring flood, the creek is just an accumulation of silt water flushing its way down to Lake Nipissing. It took us four hours of good steady paddling before we reached the last portage leading into Shoal Lake.

After dealing with the immensity of the Upper French, however, we found the small creek refreshing. With only a few signs of intrusion (ATV trails, duck blinds, and a rusted beaver trap), it happened to be one of the most isolated portions of the trip. And, to help pass the time, we kept a sharp eye out for wildlife and were greatly rewarded: beaver, muskrat and otter furrowed through the backwater; ducks of all sorts sprayed up from the clumps of sedge; and even a young black bear made a brief appearance.

Our third day was a rough one, but we were still eager to catch a feed of fish before making camp at the south end of Shoal Lake. Of course, as our luck would have it, the moment we wet our lines a fierce wind picked up from the northwest and sent us sailing across the lake. We made a couple of attempts to paddle back up the weed beds at the mouth of the north channel, but finally gave in and cooked up a bland meal of macaroni and cheese.

Day four was our shortest day en route. We traveled only from Shoal Lake to Sand Lake (also called Bass Lake) by way of Sand Creek. This was my favorite day of the trip. Sand Creek didn't twist around as much as Shoal Creek, and instead of marshland bordered by spruce and cedar, the banks were now made up of stout pine rooted atop mounds of pink granite. The 890-yard (810 m) portage into Sand Lake (Bass Lake) was interesting as well. After shouldering our packs over the trail (marked to the right of a miniature rock canyon), my partner and I decided to line the canoe up through the rapids. It wasn't as easy as taking the portage — we were able to line up the first two drops and then lift over the remaining two — but we had fun just the same.

Our group still didn't catch any fish and the cold rain started up again. But this time it didn't seem to matter as much. Peter lit another fire and then constructed an elaborate tarp, slanting it at such an angle that at times the heat became so intense we had to escape out into the rain to cool off.

The next morning was overcast and our rainjackets were put back into service as we headed out on the water. To exit Sand Lake (Bass Lake), we paddled directly south, to where the map indicated a 990-yard (900 m) portage leading overland to Watt Lake. (Yes, Watt Lake also goes by another name — Clear Lake). To the left of a swampy creek we noticed half-a-dozen aluminum boats overturned on the shore. Assuming this was the portage, we began carrying our gear along an

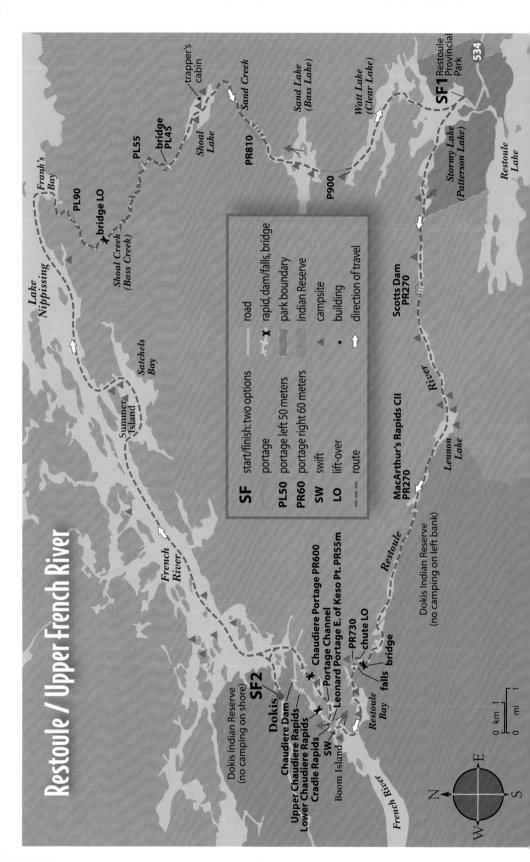

Restoule / Upper French River

unmarked trail and soon found ourselves completely lost along a network of ATV trails. The actual takeout begins further to the left and around the point.

It took us close to an hour to sort ourselves out but we eventually got all our gear over to the put-in. From here we still had a long paddle east along Watt Lake (Clear Lake) to where it joins up with the north arm of Stormy Lake (Patterson Lake) and, eventually, the familiar government docks. To us, however, completing the last portage symbolized the end of the trip more than the paddle across Watt Lake (Clear Lake). Before heading out from the trail's end we all gathered for a round of high-fives. Once again our friendship had endured the hardships of canoe tripping. We had traveled in close proximity, sharing camp chores and navigation skills, and made some difficult group decisions in some extreme conditions. Now the moment when we questioned turning back seemed distant, even shameful. In short, we were ready for next year — whatever the consequences.

The Restoule–Upper French Loop

TIME 4 to 5 days

PORTAGES 9

LONGEST PORTAGE
990 yards (900 m)

BEST TIME TO RUN IT Bass Creek dries up during the summer. It is possible to get through, but early spring or late fall is a better time to go.

FEE Since the route travels through Crown land and an unmaintained provincial park, no fee is required for Canadian citizens.

ALTERNATIVE ROUTE Try paddling it counter-clockwise, or extend your trip for two extra days by paddling around Okikendawt Island by way of the Little French River.

OUTFITTERS
North Bay Canoe Company
R.R. 2
Corbeil, Ontario
P0H 1K0
705-752-1770
www.nbcanoe.com

FOR MORE INFORMATION
Restoule Provincial Park
Restoule, Ontario
P0H 2R0
705-729-2010
1-888-668-7275 (reservations)

Ministry of Natural Resources
3301 Trout Lake Road
North Bay, Ontario
P1A 4L7
705-475-5550

MAPS The Ministry of Natural Resources has produced a pamphlet on the Restoule canoe route.

TOPOGRAPHIC MAPS
31 L/4 & 41 I/1

The French River's Old Voyageur Channel

I'VE ALWAYS WANTED TO PADDLE DOWN THE OLD VOYAGEUR CHANNEL on the lower half of the French River, not just for its sense of history but also for its reputation for smallmouth bass, walleye, pike and even monster muskie. And what better partner than Peter Fraser, a fellow angler I've gotten to know well through countless other canoe adventures.

The trip begins on the docks of Hartley Bay Marina, located at the end of Hartley Bay Road. To access the starting point turn left off Highway 69, just north of the Hungry Bear Restaurant. The put-in can be crowded, especially on a long weekend. But after you pay for your permit at the main office (located directly across the railway tracks), the marina staff will park your vehicle and help you quickly get on your way.

The route heads west along Hartley Bay for 2 miles (3 km) and then south, down Wanapitei Bay. It's best to keep to the western shoreline here, staying clear of the confusing set of islands and shallow inlets.

Ox Bay marks the most southern end of Wanapitei Bay and also where the river spreads out into a series of outlets. The Main Outlet is directly south and the Western Outlet is to the west. Take the Western Outlet, leaving the Main Outlet for your return trip back from Georgian Bay.

If you keep to the left-hand shore, it's a straightforward run from here to Crombie Bay, where the river eventually twists its way southwest. Designated campsites are marked along the way, but because this area is busy with cottage and motorboat activity, you may want to wait until just after Crombie Bay to make camp.

Peter and I pitched our tent directly on Crombie Point, and then spent a few hours exploring the old farmstead at the far southwestern point. The land was originally cleared at the turn of the century by Mr. Crombie and then later, in 1917, was settled by the King family, who worked in the local lumber camps.

You'll spend a good part of the next morning paddling an elongated stretch of the French before it splinters off into yet another set of channels, outlets and exits. To the east is the Bad River Channel, which eventually breaks off into a series of smaller outlets, all with fast swifts and boiling rapids. The Voyageur Channel is to the west and is a fairly straight passage out to Georgian Bay. However, water only flushes down this channel when river levels are high. The Old Voyageur Channel, situated between the other two outlets, was thought to be the principal route of the voyageurs and was the route of choice for Peter and me.

We first had a difficult time locating the exact entranceway to the channel, but by making good use of the detailed topographical map we packed along, Peter and I eventually began to make our way through the chasm. The further

Peter and I stop for a well-deserved break at East Cross Channel, a narrow passage navigable only by canoe.

we went along, however, the more obvious it became that only the smaller fur-trading canoes would have used this route, and even then, during high-water levels only. In particular, there are four places en route where even our light-weight, 16-foot Kevlar craft had difficulty squeezing its way through the narrow fault-line.

The first is the East Channel of the Rock Circus. Here we had to choose to navigate our craft through the area with the fewest jagged rocks; as the water level was rather low, obvious route choices became few and far between.

The next obstruction is Petite Faucille, or Little Sickle, a knee-high rock ledge just to the right of Morse Bay (a great place to fish for bass and pike). A 22-yard (20 m) portage is marked to the left, but Peter and I just lifted our gear over and then lined our canoe straight through, which is what we assumed the voyageurs had done as well. In fact, my post-trip research found that several notations of this carrying place had been written up in old journals and that

French River
Old Voyageur Channel

N
W — E
S

Legend

S start
F finish
⌒ portage
PL50 portage left 50 meters
PR60 portage right 60 meters
SW swift
LO lift-over
--- route
····· alternate route
— road
〜 rapid
▬ park boundary
▲ campsite
⟹ direction of travel

0 km .5
0 mi .5

Dispute
Island

Pig
Island

*Crombie
Bay*

Old Crombie
Farm

*French River
Western Outlet*

*French River
Western Channel*

French River
Provincial
Waterway
Park

*Voyageur
Channel*

Rock Circus

**Petite Faucill
LO or PL20**

*Old Voyageur
Channel*

Palmer Rapids
Black Bay
*Morse
Bay*

La Dalle SW

*French River
Main Outlet*

*Bad River
Channel*

Caution: Lower Bad River Channel
contains dangerous rapids, including
Back Channel, the Jump and Lily Chute

*West Cross
Channel*
**Cross Channel
Rapids**

Little Jameson Rapids PL60

Devil's Door Rapid PL50

*Sand
Bay*

Big Jameson Rapids

LO
LO

*Fort
Channel*

*East Cross
Channel*

*Whitefish
Bay*

*Gravel
Bay*

LO

Georgian Bay

Caution: Be wary of
high winds out here

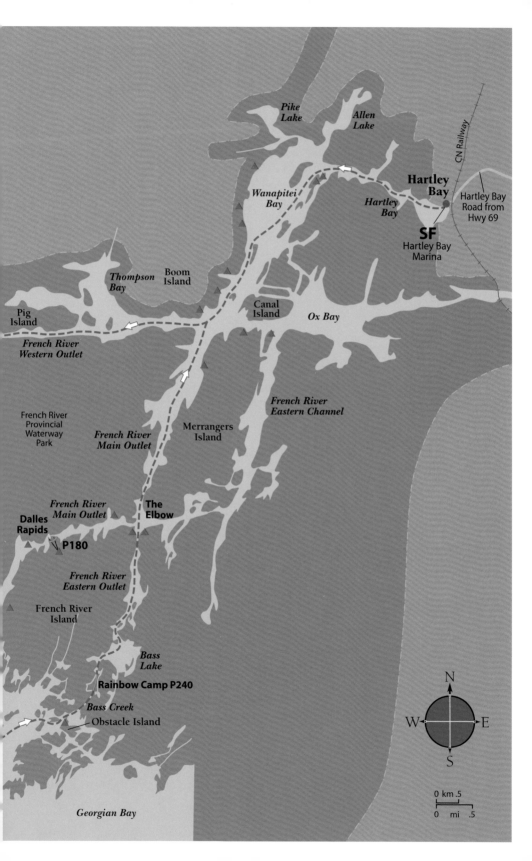

Pike Lake

Allen Lake

Hartley Bay

CN Railway

Wanapitei Bay

Hartley Bay

Hartley Bay Road from Hwy 69

SF
Hartley Bay Marina

Thompson Bay

Boom Island

Canal Island

Ox Bay

Pig Island

French River Western Outlet

French River Provincial Waterway Park

French River Eastern Channel

French River Main Outlet

Merrangers Island

French River Main Outlet

The Elbow

Dalles Rapids

P180

French River Eastern Outlet

French River Island

Bass Lake

Rainbow Camp P240

Bass Creek

Obstacle Island

Georgian Bay

N
W — E
S

0 km .5
0 mi .5

several artifacts were taken out from the base of Petite Faucille in the late 1960s. Even an 1845 painting by Paul Kane, titled *French River Rapid*, is thought to be of voyageurs portaging around the same location.

Two noteworthy sections remain — Palmer Rapids and La Dalle — both located not far downstream from Petite Faucille. A series of angled rocks can make Palmer Rapids difficult in low or moderate water, but La Dalle is no problem at any water level.

Once past La Dalle, the river flows into what is called the West Cross Channel. From here the voyageurs had two ways to reach the expanse of Georgian Bay: travel west on the same channel or paddle directly out by way of the Fort Channel. Of course, Peter and I chose neither. We were traveling east, back toward our vehicles at Hartley Bay. We made sure to keep close to the right shoreline so as not to get lost while traveling up the West Cross Channel; this was especially important just before we lined up the Cross Channel Rapids. By discovering a few dead ends along the way and asking the odd boater for directions, we eventually found ourselves at the base of the three cascades emptying out of the Bad River — Back Channel, the Jump, and Lily Chute.

Other anglers had gathered here to fish, so Peter and I took time out to jig for walleye. The spot looked ideal, but we caught only a couple of perch. An hour later the sun was close to setting, and with more boats beginning to gather, it seemed a prime time to fish the rapids. But we had yet to set up camp and decided to continue on to a protective cove just east of the Devil's Door Rapid.

At low water the Devil's Door was easy to run. I could well imagine, however, that during spring runoff it would be next to impossible. There is a short portage to the north, but because of its location, it doesn't seem safe at all. I would rather line or run Big Jameson, located directly to the south, or even make use of Little Jameson's portage, which is marked at the end of the inlet to the right of the Devil's Door.

Peter and I were amazed at how crowded the harbor was just beyond the Devil's Door; an assortment of fancy speedboats, yachts and outboard runabouts had moored for the night at the same place we had planned on staying. It's not that we expected to be totally alone while out on the Bay. We just never thought that we'd have to camp alongside of them. But Peter and I made the best of it by pitching our tent behind some trees, trying to ignore the humming of generators and the crackle of short-wave radios.

The next morning Peter and I made the decision to stay clear of the crowds by following the East Cross Channel, a narrow passage navigable only by canoe. At first the route was straightforward enough. But by mid-morning we had lifted over two large beaver dams, waded through a number of rocky shallows, and become "confused" about our location at least half-a-dozen times. The bottom of our canoe suffered greatly, but we neither saw nor heard another boat.

Georgian Bay was surprisingly calm when we finally reached it, and Peter and I took advantage of the openness by paddling far out past the reefs to troll for a monster pike. At one point we even thought seriously of making the crossing to the Bustard Islands — a collection of 559 rocks over 2 miles (3 km) out from the mainland.

The group of islands — named after a European game bird that made a habit of frequenting isolated areas — has long been a favorite anchorage for boats traveling out on Georgian Bay. The most popular stopover is the Bustard Island Lighthouse. The navigation beacon was first manned in 1875 by Edward B. Barron, who, surprisingly enough, was a canoeist. Besides his commission at the lighthouse, the keeper was hired by the government to make exploratory trips to the James Bay area by way of canoe.

Peter and I had reached about the halfway point when we felt a breath of wind blow across the water. That was all we needed to make us come to our senses and head back for shore. The canoe rose easily on the waves at first, but as we approached the mouth of the Main Channel the breeze had turned into a steady gale. The boat began to tip and wobble in the troughs. Luckily, my wife, Alana, and I had traveled in the same area a year earlier and found ourselves in a similar dilemma. We had escaped by finding shelter in a circuit of islands and coves not far to the east, so Peter and I decided to make a run for it.

The islands seemed close enough, but midway across, the winds were steadily building and our canoe began to take on water. To help brace, we both jammed our knees tight against the gunwales and headed further downwind. That lengthened the distance but seemed to keep us drier. Eventually we glided into flat, calm waters and made camp on the lee side of Obstacle Island.

The winds had made us nervous of Georgian Bay, and the next day we found ourselves on the water quite early. Taking full advantage of the morning lull, we quietly escaped back upriver by way of the Eastern Outlet's Bass Creek Tramway. This 262-yard-long (240 m) boardwalk, originally constructed of rails mounted on large timbers, was first established as a way for the lumber companies, which were phasing out operations at French River Village (just below Dalles Rapids), to move their mills elsewhere out on Georgian Bay. The skidway has been rebuilt over the years and used for a number of purposes, from transporting firefighting equipment for the Department of Lands and Forests to providing a shortcut to the Bay for boaters and canoeists. A cluster of cabins at the end of the tramway marks the remains of Rainbow Camp, one of the first of many bustling fishing lodges that operated along the French River in the early 1900s.

From the put-in at Rainbow Camp, the route heads across to the northeast of Bass Lake. From there, it continues up the Eastern Outlet, to the intersection with the Main Outlet called the Elbow, and then directly up the Main Outlet to the familiar Wanapitei Bay.

Peter and I took time out to fish while paddling this entire stretch. It had rained on us since Bass Lake, but we figured the change of weather would bring on the fish — and we were right. By the time we reached Ox Bay we had caught a mess of pike — the biggest weighing in at 16 pounds. The rain, though, had now changed to a constant downpour and a lather of whitecaps formed across the water.

Once again we made the right choice by heading for shore. We immediately set up camp. It took only minutes for us to erect the tent and tie down the canoe, but by then hurricane winds had whipped the water into a frenzy and we could hear nearby trees snapping like matchsticks.

The skies quickly darkened overhead. Peter and I ran for the relative safety of our flimsy nylon tarp to watch as great forks of lightning set the air crackling with electricity. We were a bit shaken by the event but, except for a soggy tent (Peter forgot to zip up the front flap), we came out of it unharmed. Little did we know, however, that a twister had touched down nearby, forcing two men to swim almost 100 yards back to shore after their house was tossed into the lake by a funnel cloud. Oblivious to the nearby destruction, we mourned the loss of dry sleeping bags and a good night's sleep, then headed back to the marina the next morning.

The French River's Old Voyageur's Channel

TIME 4 to 5 days

DIFFICULTY Perfect for the novice canoeist. Just watch out for the heavy winds on Georgian Bay.

PORTAGES 3

LONGEST PORTAGE
262 yards (240 m)

BEST TIME TO RUN IT
Spring through fall

FEE The French River is an unmaintained provincial park, and no camping fee is required for canoeing the river. However, a fee is charged to park your vehicle at the Hartley Bay Marina.

ALTERNATIVE ROUTE The route can be extended by continuing east along Georgian Bay and loop back to Wanapitei Bay by way of the Pickerel River.

OUTFITTERS
Grundy Lake Supply Post
R.R. 1, Hwy. 69 & Hwy. 522
Britt, Ontario
P0G 1A0
705-383-2251

FOR MORE INFORMATION
Ministry of Natural Resources
3767 Hwy. 69 S.
Sudbury, Ontario
P3G 1E7
705-564-7823

MAPS The Ministry of Natural Resources has produced a canoe route map for the entire French River.

TOPOGRAPHIC MAPS
41 I/2, 41 H/14 & 41 H/15

The Mattawa River

I HAVE TO GIVE THE GANG AT BOSTON MILLS PRESS a lot of credit, especially editor Noel Hudson. Noel has read over every misadventure I've ever had in a canoe. Yet not only does he still agree to tag along with the rest of my publishing company on our annual paddling trip, he chooses to be my canoe partner as well. Of course, things haven't always been so bad for Noel. He has had only to deal with his prize lake trout being accidentally tenderized when I tied it from the back end of the canoe during a long portage in Algonquin. Then there was that slight concussion I gave him when the rock wrapped around the end of the bear rope came loose as I tossed it over the limb of a tree. But then last year, during our first river adventure, Noel and I went sideways down a chute at Portage de la Prairie on the Mattawa River. Believe it or not, however, he's my partner again this season, and I'm starting to wonder if Noel actually trusts me or he just keeps drawing the short straw back at the office.

The trip started off innocently enough. We all met in the town of Mattawa and then had Fudge Doucette at the Petro-Canada gas station on McConnell Drive (just across the road from the town's tourism building) shuttle us back up to the top end of the river. We took Highway 17 and, deciding to bypass Trout Lake so as to begin directly at the entrance to the Mattawa Waterway Park, turned right at Corbeil Corners (Highway 94) on Centennial Drive. From there we followed MacPherson Drive almost 4 miles (6 km) to the road's end.

After loading the canoes at the government docks, we headed east and paddled through the narrows to the left, passing the historic Portage de la Tortue. Originally there was a shallow, rocky section here that Natives, explorers, missionaries and voyageurs had to carry around when traveling on the Mattawa. The obstruction was later blasted open to connect Trout Lake and Turtle Lake.

At the end of Turtle Lake there's a choice of two routes that will take you to Talon Lake — the largest lake en route. You can keep with the river and make use of five portages (none of which measures over 165 yards [150 m]), or continue east and portage in and out of Pine Lake. We chose the second of the two (the traditional route of the voyageurs), hoping to spend our first night out on one of the islands of Pine Lake.

So we paddled up a muddy creek (which, oddly, drains in the opposite direction as the Mattawa), lifted over a beaver dam, made use of the 220-yard (200 m) Portage de la Mauvaise Musique on the right, and then set up camp on the north side of Pine Lake's largest island.

Portage Pin de Musique, 490 yards (450 m) long and marked in a weedy bay to the northeast, led us out of Pine Lake and into Talon Lake's McCool Bay the next morning. The wind was coming from the northwest, but caused us some concern only while paddling toward the far point off to the right. As soon as we rounded the corner, we were able to speed down to Talon Chutes at the southeast end.

Portage de Talon (named after the governor of New France, Jean Talon) is one of the most difficult portages en route. Marked to the right, just before a dam, the 360-yard (330 m) trail makes its way over a series of precarious rock ridges and then descends steeply down toward a small beach. Of course, thinking back to when the voyageurs carried monstrous packs weighing no less than 180 pounds, a modern-day canoeist burdened down with lightweight canoes and packs shouldn't really complain.

Difficult portages aside, Talon Chutes is an incredibly historic place. Natives held vision quests in the 6-to-16-foot-deep potholes scoured out of the rock on the north side; a section of the 100-foot-high (30 m) cliff below the chutes was used as a lookout when the invading Iroquois ambushed the Nippissing people. A rock formation above the potholes, called the Dog Face, appeared in Ripley's *Believe It or Not* in the 1950s. Well-known canoeist and cinematographer Bill Mason shot footage here for the portage scene in his film *The Voyageurs*. And William and Jacques, the two characters from the popular television commercials for Labatt's Brewery, jumped off the south side of the chute. (Jacques lost his wig on the first take, and the whole scene had to be redone.)

Not far downstream, just before the river empties into Pimisi Bay, is another historic gem — a humpbacked rock on the north bank called the Watchdog. There, Natives and voyageurs left an offering of tobacco to appease the spirits and ensure safe passage. Noel and I should have taken heed of this, for it was on the third set of the five upcoming rapids where we took our ill-fated dump.

The first rapid begins where the river heads north out of Pimisi Bay. A 165-yard (150 m) portage is on the right. It's called Descharge des Perches, being the place where the voyageurs discarded their poles used for traveling upstream. We all ran through, rushing over the remains of an old logging dam and then down the left channel of a rocky Class I rapid (be ready to make a sharp right turn at the bottom).

The second rapid, with an unnamed 220-yard (200 m) portage found at the end of the small bay on the southeast side, as well as the third set, with the 110-yard (100 m) Portage de la Cave marked on the left, were far more difficult Class Is. We still managed to run them, however, with a tight squeeze between the rocks near the bottom of the third set being the most challenging part.

Then, after heading down a quick swift (there's an unnecessary 55-yard [50 m] portage on the right), we approached the last run before Paresseux Falls. Everyone headed for the 316-yard (287 m) Portage de la Prairie (also known as Petite Paresseux) marked on the left — everyone except Noel and me, of course. I'm not sure if it was arrogance, laziness [Editor's note: *paresseux* does mean

Kathy and Mary stop to explore Porte de L'Enfer, just one of the many historic sites found along the Mattawa River.

Mattawa River

Camp Conewango
Outfitter **S3**

Lake

Talon

P450
Portage Pin de Musique

*McCool
Bay*
island sites

Pine Lake

**Portage de la Mauvaise Musique
PR200**

beaver dam LO

PR50

PR150

PR150

PR150

PR50

*Turtle
Lake*

17

island site

Mattawa River Provincial
Waterway Park

Portage de la Tortue
(no longer used)

S1

MacPherson
Drive

Centennial
Drive

94

**Corbeil
Corners**

17

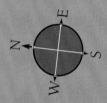

S	start: five options
F	finish
⌒	portage
PL50	portage left 50 meters
PR60	portage right 60 meters
SW	swift
LO	lift-over
– – –	route
･･･････	alternate route
────	road
⌇⌇	rapid, dam/falls
▓▓	park boundary
▲	campsite
➡	direction of travel

*Trout

Lake*

F2 Armstrong
Beach

63

11

North Bay

0 km 1
0 mi 1

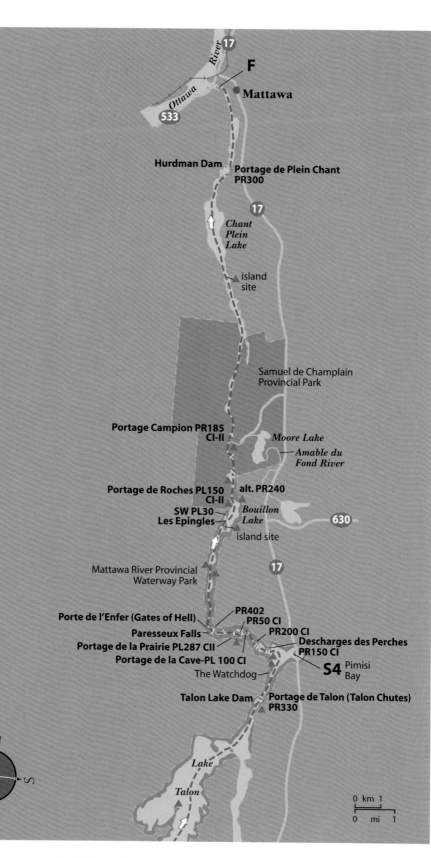

"lazy"] or just plain stupidity, but I suggested to Noel that we run down the first drop and have a look at what was around the corner. What a mistake!

Halfway down we found ourselves caught up in the current and tried to power toward shore. That failed miserably. Then we tried to eddy in behind a small boulder. That also failed. And it wasn't long before we found ourselves drifting sideways to the current, heading toward a miniature fall.

It wasn't a dramatic flip. Noel and I just slid sideways down a smooth piece of rock, miraculously staying upright until the very end. There was a brief moment of panic when Noel's foot became wedged in a rock and held him under, but he eventually recovered and we began swimming downriver after our packs and canoe. Miraculously, the only item lost was Noel's favorite baseball cap.

The rest of the group, who all had safely walked around the rapid, arrived at the put-in just in time to witness us coming ashore, looking like a couple of drowned rats. I don't think they had much sympathy for us, but they did point out that there was a campsite halfway along the portage if we wanted to stop for the day. Noel and I refused, however, and insisted that they just allow us time to change into some dry clothes before continuing on. It was a humbling experience, to say the least.

The 26-foot-high Paresseux Falls, with a mandatory 440-yard (402 m) portage on the right, is absolutely breathtaking. What's even more impressive, however, is Porte de L'Enfer — a narrow cave located just around the corner on the north side of the river.

The site is actually an old Native mining site dating back 3,000 years. Lured here by the sounds of spirits singing at the base of the falls, the Native people found the rich veins of hematite, an oxide of iron that when refined was used as the basis for the rock paintings known as pictographs. The superstitious voyageurs, however, interpreted this as the living quarters for a flesh-eating demon (its blood made up of the red ochre), and named it the "Gates of Hell."

The first campsite after Paresseux Falls is where our group stayed for our last night on the river. In the morning, Noel and I, wary from our dump the day before, had to be seduced out of our tent by the smell of bacon, eggs and fresh coffee.

The first rapid of the day, Les Epingles, was a mere swift leading into Bouillion Lake. Noel and I regained a bit of confidence by making a clear run down the center (a 33-yard [30 m] portage does exist on the left). After one look at the rapids flowing out on the other end of Bouillion Lake — a Class I-II that had become quite technical due to the low water levels — we panicked, however, and headed straight for the 165-yard (150 m) Portage de Roches marked on the left (for some reason there is also a portage, 262 yards [240 m] long, on the right).

Portage Campion, measuring 202 yards (185 m) and found on the right (just past where the Amable du Fond River, coming from the upper reaches of Algonquin Park, enters the Mattawa), marks the next set of rapids. Noel and I scouted the set first, and classed it as another technical Class I-II. But since it was the last navigable whitewater of our trip, we convinced ourselves it was safe

"Kevin, how many more portages before we make camp?" John and James, complaining again, at Talon Chutes.

to run. So, after talking over our planned route (starting center and then going a tad to the right to avoid most of the shallow stuff), we ran it not only once, but three times.

Portage Campion also marks the river access to Samuel de Champlain Provincial Park. This makes for an excellent alternative take-out point, especially since the Mattawa Waterway Provincial Park ends soon after the provincial campground and cottage development begins to appear just before the Hurdman Dam. (A 330-yard [300 m] portage — Portage de Plein Chant — is marked to the right of the dam.) The traditional end point, however, is in the town of Mattawa, at a municipal park located on the south side of the river just before the cement bridge. We chose the customary route, basically because that's where our shuttle driver had stored our vehicles. The extra three-hour paddle was worth it, though. The section before Hurdman Dam, where the river spreads itself into a placid sheet and surrounds itself with high walls of granite, was quite scenic. You may enjoy a sense of history by ending at the confluence of the Mattawa and Ottawa Rivers (Mattawa is actually the Ojibwa word for "meeting of the waters"). We enjoyed the poutine and cold drinks we bought at a restaurant on the main street of Mattawa. And by storing our vehicles back at the Petro-Canada gas bar and not having to pay for parking at Samuel de Champlain Provincial Park, I was able to save enough money in the end to buy poor Noel another baseball cap and a comical pair of water wings to match.

TIME 3 to 4 days

DIFFICULTY This is a novice route, since all rapids come with well-marked portages.

PORTAGES 13

LONGEST PORTAGE
490 yards (450 m)

BEST TIME TO RUN IT
Spring through fall

FEE No interior camping permit is required for Mattawa Provincial Park. A moderate shuttle fee is required, however.

ALTERNATIVE ROUTE By starting out at North Bay's Armstrong Park, on Lakeside Drive just off Trout Lake Road (Highway 63), you can add an extra few hours of paddling across Trout Lake.

OUTFITTERS
Fudge Doucette
Mattawa Petro-Canada
290 McConnell Drive
Box 774
Mattawa, Ontario
P0H 1V0
705-744-2866

Valley Ventures
Box 1115
Deep River, Ontario
K0J 1P0
613-584-2577
www.magma.ca

Draper's Wilderness Adventures
510 Valios Drive
Box 247
Mattawa, Ontario
P0H 1V0
705-744-2323
www.gdraper.com

North Bay Canoe Company
R.R. 2
Corbeil, Ontario
P0H 1K0
705-474-6634
www.nbcanoe.com

FOR MORE INFORMATION
Samuel de Champlain
  Provincial Park
1-888-668-7275 (reservations)
or
Friends of the Mattawa River
  Heritage Park
Box 147
Mattawa, Ontario
P0H 1V0
705-744-2276

MAPS The Friends of the Mattawa River Heritage Park have produced a very detailed canoe map for the Mattawa River. Hap Wilson's guidebook, *Rivers of the Upper Ottawa Valley: Myth, Magic and Adventure*, is also an excellent resource. You can also refer to the Mattawa River map in The Adventure Map series by Chrismar.

TOPOGRAPHIC MAPS
31 L/6 & 31 L/7

The Temagami River

NOT ALL CANOE PARTNERS ARE PERFECTLY MATCHED when it comes to river running. Look at Mark van Stempvoort and me. He's a fanatic when it comes to playing in the rapids; the more technical the better. For me, it's a different story. If there's even the slightest chance of going for a swim, I head for the portage. That's why the Temagami River was perfect for the two of us. There are plenty of Class II and III rapids for Mark to test his skill out on and many well-trodden portages for me to use as escape routes.

Mark and I organized our own car shuttle by both driving to the route's end in River Valley, a small hamlet along Highway 539A, north of the town of Field. Here we parked Mark's vehicle on the south side of the river bridge and to the left of the roadway, and then drove back toward Field, heading east off Highway 64 and north on Highway 11. Eventually we turned left onto the Central Lake Temagami Access Road, about 3.75 miles (6 km) south of the town of Temagami.

From the government dock we paddled south, stopping on the east shore of High Rock Island to hike up to a fabulous lookout. From this vantage point Mark and I could see far out across the wild expanse of Lake Temagami's skyline reserve. We quickly came to realize why, even as far back as the late 1800s, recreational canoeists have visited the Temagami area, preferring it over the much "tamer" Algonquin region.

After our short break we continued on southward, entering Portage Bay to search out a set of Native pictographs on the lower east side. Then we made use of the 27-yard (25 m) portage that gives the bay its name to head back out into the main portion of Temagami Lake. From here we turned toward the southeastern outlet to paddle through the S-Narrows (a place where Natives once speared woodland caribou where they gathered to cross the channel), took the left channel where the waterway forks (the right channel is shorter but can become unnavigable in low-water conditions), and then stopped for our first night on Cross Lake.

The next day, after paddling to the southern end of Surveyor Lake, which is really an extension of Cross Lake, Mark and I encountered the first real portage of the trip. The 286-yard (260 m) trail begins to the left of a control dam and comes complete with an incredibly steep put-in as well as a quick set of rapids at the bottom.

The swift water continues past Cross Lake Dam with a series of intermediate rapids. The first, a triple Class III that's found not far downstream from where an old logging bridge once spanned the river, is the most challenging. Mark and I, wanting to first scout the entire set, carried our packs over the

A logger's grave below Island Falls.

660-yard (600 m) portage on the left, and then walked up along the shoreline to get a closer look.

It took us a good half hour before we were both convinced of a safe route down all three drops, and even when we did run down the rapid, Mark and I took full advantage of every possible eddy to slow down and take time to firm up our next move.

We managed to complete each of our preplanned maneuvers, but overall it was a stressful run, particularly a close encounter with dangerous hydraulics billowing up from below the second drop. That is why we were surprised to see the leader of eight cedar canvas canoes filled with greenhorn camp kids (who, we discovered later, were beginning a one-month expedition to James Bay) simply stand up in his canoe to scout the same rapid, and then yell out, "Looks fine from here, boys." Down they went, with only two of the eight canoes still upright at the bottom.

Of course, after they had bailed the water out of their boats and gathered their totally soaked belongings, you'd think the leader would have directed them toward shore. Not this guy. He just blindly led them down the next rapid (a technical Class II), taking little if any notice of the well-used 197-yard (180 m) portage marked on the left bank. This time, all the canoeists dumped, including the leader himself.

Not far downstream, a 550-yard (500 m) portage, marked to the left, avoids a triple set of rapids. The first drop is an easy run, however. So only the second and third (a dangerous chute and shallow technical set) have to be carried around, reducing the portage to 275 yards (250 m).

Only two smaller rapids remain before Cedar Lake. The second has an unnecessary 190-yard (175 m) portage on the left. Mark and I set up camp at a luxurious site well hidden from the few cottages nearby. It was only one of two possible sites on Cedar Lake, however, and we were forced to clean the firepit of beer cans and scavenge the backwoods for suitable firewood before we could cook up our evening meal — salmon couscous with tortilla cinnamon rolls for dessert.

The route continues to the southern tip of Cedar Lake where a short, 190-yard (175 m) portage to the left of the outlet dam takes you into Thistle Lake. In my opinion, it's a much nicer lake than Red Cedar Lake, with more exposed rock outcrops and even a few sandy beaches where you can set up camp. Then, a little ways beyond three short swifts at the west outlet of Thistle Lake, you must use a 130-yard (120 m) portage on the left to avoid a difficult set of rapids. (An alternative portage, measuring 110 yards [100 m], is also on the right bank.)

Not long after, the river takes a dramatic turn to the north and flushes over two moderate rapids. The first runs left, right and center of a small island. The government map shows a 220-yard (200 m) portage on the east bank. Mark and I, however, could find only a rough, unmarked trail leading across the center island, so we decided to navigate down the far right channel (a Class II), which happened to have the most water running through it.

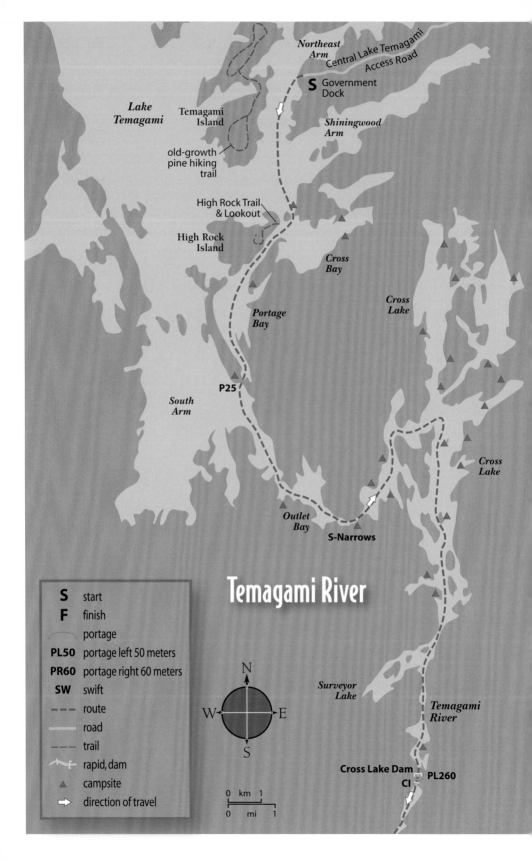

Temagami River

Northeast Arm

Central Lake Temagami

Access Road

S Government Dock

Lake Temagami

Temagami Island

old-growth pine hiking trail

Shiningwood Arm

High Rock Trail & Lookout

High Rock Island

Cross Bay

Cross Lake

Portage Bay

P25

South Arm

Cross Lake

Outlet Bay

S-Narrows

Surveyor Lake

Temagami River

Cross Lake Dam
Cl **PL260**

S	start
F	finish
	portage
PL50	portage left 50 meters
PR60	portage right 60 meters
SW	swift
	route
	road
	trail
	rapid, dam
▲	campsite
→	direction of travel

N
W — E
S

0   km   1
0   mi   1

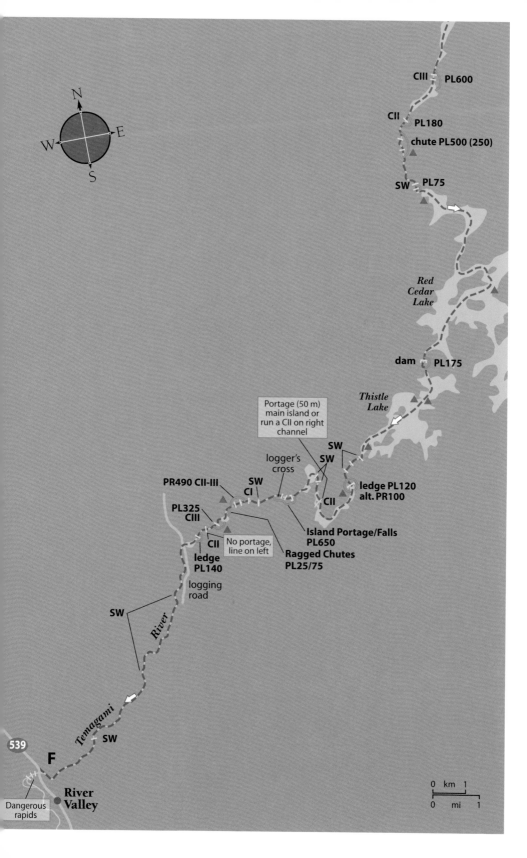

CIII PL600

CII PL180

chute PL500 (250)

SW PL75

Red Cedar Lake

dam PL175

Thistle Lake

Portage (50 m) main island or run a CII on right channel

logger's cross

SW
SW

SW
CI

PR490 CII-III

ledge PL120
alt. PR100

CII

PL325
CIII

Island Portage/Falls
PL650

No portage,
line on left

Ragged Chutes
PL25/75

CII
ledge
PL140

logging
road

SW

River

539

Temagami

SW

F

River Valley

Dangerous
rapids

0   km   1

0   mi   1

The second rapid — a double swift with a good standing wave at the bottom — occurs just before the river bends back to the west. Keep to the left shoreline here to stay south of another island.

Island Portage (710 yards [650 m] and marked on the left) is the most difficult carry en route, not only for its ruggedness, but also because of its confusing network of side trails and various put-in spots. Make sure to stay right directly past the take-out (the left trail leads who knows where) and head up a steep hill. Then, after series of muddy hollows, keep to the trail as it makes its way along the river and eventually levels out before the proper put-in.

Mark and I, glad to have finished the grueling portage, decided to paddle upriver to enjoy lunch and a swim at the base of the twin chutes we had just carried around. On the way we took time out to snap a couple of photos of a logger's grave marked by a wooden cross high on top the north bank.

Next, downriver and just past a small swift and a quick Class I, is a serious drop that must be portaged 540 yards (490 m) on the right. Mark and I camped for our last night at a site three-quarters of the way along the trail, and then spent the afternoon practicing our whitewater skills on the lower half of the rapids — rated a technical Class II or Class III.

Ragged Chutes, consisting of two major drops, comes almost immediately after the last rapid. First you must portage 27 yards (25 m) on the left to a small lagoon. Then, either line your canoe along the steep rocky bank or carefully run the short stretch of rapids before taking out and portaging another 80 yards (75 m) on the left.

Three more rapids follow close after Ragged Chutes. For the first set, Mark and I carried our gear over the 358-yard (325 m) portage on the left and then ran the rapid empty. The second had no portage, but there were some big rocks down the center, and Mark and I ended up lining a good section of it. And the last set was a large chute that only suicidal playboaters would attempt, so we used the 153-yard (140 m) portage marked on the left.

Once past a bridge, the Temagami River flows swiftly but without any real rapids for a total of 3.75 miles (6 km). Including a half-hour lunch break beside a herd of neighborhood cows, it took Mark and me only two hours to reach River Valley.

The take-out spot is to the right, just before the 539A bridge. It's a steep climb up the eroded bank, and at first glance the rapids just beyond the bridge don't seem all that difficult. Don't be fooled, however! The rapids end in a small falls just past a railway bridge. Once you've entered the fast water, it's almost impossible to bail out.

TIME 4 to 5 days

DIFFICULTY
A good intermediate trip

PORTAGES 15

LONGEST PORTAGE
710 yards (650 m)

BEST TIME TO RUN IT The Temagami River is dam controlled and can usually be run spring through fall.

FEE The route travels through Crown land, where no fee is required for Canadian citizens. There may be a charge for shuttling your vehicle.

ALTERNATIVE ROUTE The rapids below Red Cedar Lake are more difficult than those in the upper section, so novice canoeists may wish to link back to Lake Temagami from Red Cedar by a series of small lakes to the northeast.

OUTFITTERS
Smoothwater Outdoor Center
Box 40
Temagami, Ontario
P0H 2H0
705-569-3539
www.smoothwater.com

Temagami Wilderness Center Limited
R.R. 1
Temagami, Ontario
P0H 2H0
705-569-3733
www.temagami.com

Temagami Outfitting Company
Box 512, 20 Lakeshore Drive
Temagami, Ontario
P0H 2H0
705-569-2595
www.icanoe.ca

FOR MORE INFORMATION
Ministry of Natural Resources
3301 Trout Lake Road
North Bay, Ontario
P1A 4L7
705-475-5550

MAPS The Ministry of Natural Resources have produced a canoe map for the Temagami District. Hap Wilson's guidebook, *Temagami Canoe Routes*, is also an excellent resource.

TOPOGRAPHIC MAPS
41 I/16, 31 L/13, 31L/12 & 41 I/9 Provincial Series Maps: Scale 1:100,000 Capreol 41 I/NE & Tomiko 31 L/MW

Temagami's Sturgeon River

IT WAS THE CHANCE TO HIKE UP THE SCENIC ISHPATINA RIDGE — the highest point in Ontario — that brought me to Temagami's Sturgeon River. The river itself was just a way to paddle back after being flown in to the trailhead on Scarecrow Lake. When all was said and done, though, it was the route home that impressed me the most. With its seemingly endless Class I and II rapids, abundant wildlife, constantly changing scenery and remote setting, I'd have to say that the Sturgeon River is one of the best trips Ontario's Temagami District has to offer.

It takes at least seven days to paddle from Scarecrow Lake back to Lakeland Airway's home base in Temagami, located on the left of Highway 11. An even quicker and cheaper way, however, is to have the pilot pick you up on Wawiagama Lake, saving you two strenuous days of paddling across the expanse of Obabika Lake and Temagami Lake.

To drive to Wawiagama Lake, turn off Highway 17 and onto Highway 64, just west of the town of Sturgeon Falls. Then, once at the town of Field, go over the river bridge and stay left, following 539A to the town of River Valley. From here the road eventually turns into 805. It's a gravel road, not a highway, and passes by a makeshift trailer-park alongside Emerald Lake. Just beyond here the main road ends and the drive becomes somewhat adventurous. (You should seriously consider the extra two days of paddling to the town docks in Temagami if your vehicle is not suitable for backroad driving.)

After 4.5 miles (7 km) the dirt road forks. Go right and follow an even rougher bush road for another 3 miles (5.6 km). Just before a metal gate, turn left and drive into a logging camp. Behind the buildings to your left is a trail leading down to Wawiagama Lake. The pilot will land at a scheduled time and wait for you out in the middle of the lake. Simply paddle out and climb aboard.

Greg was my pilot. He had worked for Lakeland Airways for two years, making about twenty flights into Scarecrow, but never from Wawiagama Lake. It was a twenty-five minute flight to Scarecrow and Greg took the time to fly over Ishpatina Ridge to show me the trail leading up to the fire tower. He then landed in the center of the lake (the bay to the north was too shallow to let me off directly at the trailhead) and, being a typical bush pilot, had my gear unloaded and his plane back in the air in a matter of seconds — leaving me adrift and totally alone.

The pure solitude always overpowers me at first. To relieve the butterflies bouncing around in my gut, I tend to keep myself busy. The Sturgeon River trip was no exception. Right off I headed for the lookout trail. The hike to the top of Ishpatina Ridge took me just over an hour and a half. Except for two main steep sections — one halfway along and the other a half hour from the summit, just after a small pond — the climb was more gradual than I thought. The experience itself wasn't all that memorable for me, however. The bush along the way was thick with mosquitoes, brought on by an approaching thunderstorm. I reached the top the moment the storm hit and, figuring that the highest point in Ontario wasn't the safest place to be during a lightning strike, I snapped a total of three pictures and scrambled back down the trail.

It was 2 p.m. by the time I got back to my canoe. I guess I should have made camp on Scarecrow (there's a great island campsite at the south end). But the rain had stopped, and not yet feeling a part of my surroundings, I still felt this strange urgency to keep moving.

From Scarecrow I headed south and entered Woods Lake by way of a small swift. At the far end of the lake was my first portage — a 153-yard (140 m) trail marked to the right of a dilapidated rock dam. It was a short carry but the clouds of mosquitoes waiting for me at the take-out made me curse the detour. The bugs were even worse at the small pond just past the put-in and I was forced to wear a bug net while I navigated down three shallow rapids.

Another small rapid follows a second pond and then, once past an old bridge, where you may have to lift over on the left if logs are blocking the way, Hamlow Lake comes into view. From Hamlow there are three route choices to reach the Sturgeon River. The first is to paddle to the northwest and take a 182-yard (165 m) portage to Stull Lake (marked approximately 55 yards [50 m] beyond a bush road), and then follow a 2,062-yard (1,875 m) portage at the extreme west end of Stull Lake, marked directly across from another bush road.

Ishpatina Ridge, the highest point in Ontario.

The second option is to portage an old logging road found in the southeast bay of Hamlow Lake, near an old mill site. And the last choice is to follow Stull Creek flowing out of the far end of Hamlow Lake.

All three routes have their difficulties. The 2,062-yard (1,875 m) portage from Stull Lake makes its way through swamps and a large burned-over area; the logging road is 2 miles (3 km) in length; and the creek can become almost unnavigable during low water.

But since it was the middle of June, I opted for Stull Creek. In the two hours it took me to reach the river, I found myself carrying across seven short but very steep unmarked portages (including one on the west side of a 10-foot-high waterfall) and dragging over countless boulder fields and logjams. In short, it would be impossible to explain paddling this ill-fated stream in any great detail, so I'll leave you to your own navigation skills. Just take it slow, curse a lot, and remember what canoeist and filmmaker Robert Perkins said while attempting to paddle down a drainage tunnel leading under the town of Oxford, England: "You know, they said I couldn't do this. But the idea isn't to do it; the idea is to try to do it. If you try, you might get it done." Of course, he never made it, but you get the point.

It was already 7 p.m. when I reached the Sturgeon River. But I spent another hour running a series of shallow rapids (one before the old logging road and three more sets below it) before making camp on Paul Lake. I pulled up on a steep rock outcrop and immediately removed my boots to wring out my wet socks. My white feet, sodden and wrinkled like prunes, enjoyed their freedom — that is, until the mosquitoes found the newly exposed skin. So, after a quick dinner of peanut butter and jam sandwiches, I escaped into my tent and didn't crawl out until late the next morning.

An impressive high wall of rock at the far end of Paul Lake squeezes the river back to its original form, creating three minor swifts before it empties out into Ghoul Lake. The route continues south from here, passing a 1,518-yard (1,380 m) portage on the left that heads into the Solace Lake Provincial Waterway Park. The Solace Lake region was one of three waterway parks, the Obabika and Sturgeon River Parks being the other two, that were established in the battle to return Temagami to a wilderness state; this new parkland added 65,900 acres to the already huge, 178,900-acre (72,400 ha) Lady Evelyn Provincial Park to the north.

The Sturgeon River route, however, continues south across Ghoul Lake. The take-out for the 275-yard (250 m) Twin Falls portage is marked to the far right by a prime campsite. The portage heads over bedrock behind the campsite and then straight down a steep slope, ending directly beside a second but smaller falls to the right.

The current speeds up greatly after Twin Falls, with two short but rocky rapids before Eaglenest Lake, and eleven more before you reach Lyman Lake and Kettle Falls. The whole run is a blast — except if the water is low — and only the second and seventh set past Eaglenest Lake have to be checked out

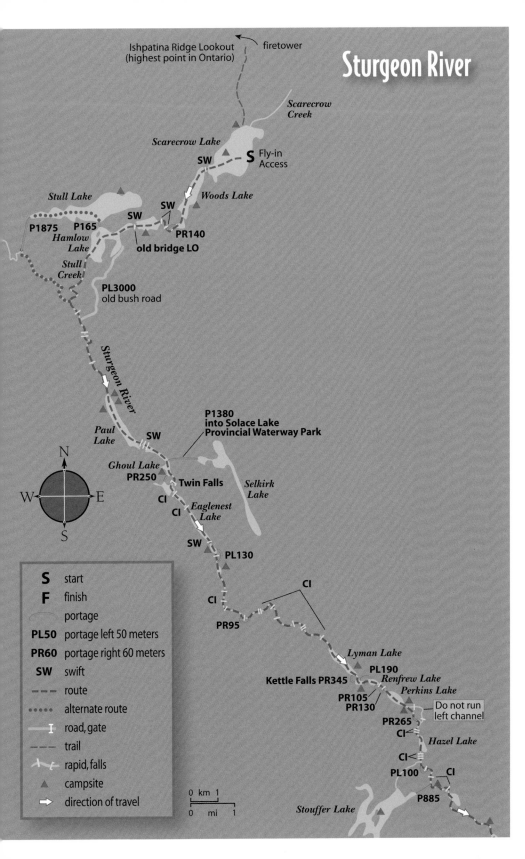

Sturgeon River

Ishpatina Ridge Lookout
(highest point in Ontario)
firetower

Scarecrow
Creek

Scarecrow Lake

SW **S** Fly-in
Access

Woods Lake

SW

SW

Stull Lake

P1875 **P165** SW

*Hamlow
Lake*

PR140

old bridge LO

*Stull
Creek*

PL3000
old bush road

Sturgeon River

*Paul
Lake* SW

Ghoul Lake

PR250 **Twin Falls**

CI *Eaglenest
Lake*

CI

SW

PL130

**P1380
into Solace Lake
Provincial Waterway Park**

*Selkirk
Lake*

CI

CI

PR95

Lyman Lake

PL190

Kettle Falls PR345 *Renfrew Lake*

PR105 *Perkins Lake*

PR130 Do not run
left channel

PR265

CI *Hazel Lake*

CI

PL100 CI

P885

Stouffer Lake

S start
F finish
⁀ portage
PL50 portage left 50 meters
PR60 portage right 60 meters
SW swift
- - - route
•••• alternate route
——I— road, gate
—— trail
↟↟↟ rapid, falls
▲ campsite
➡ direction of travel

N
W E
S

0 km 1
0 mi 1

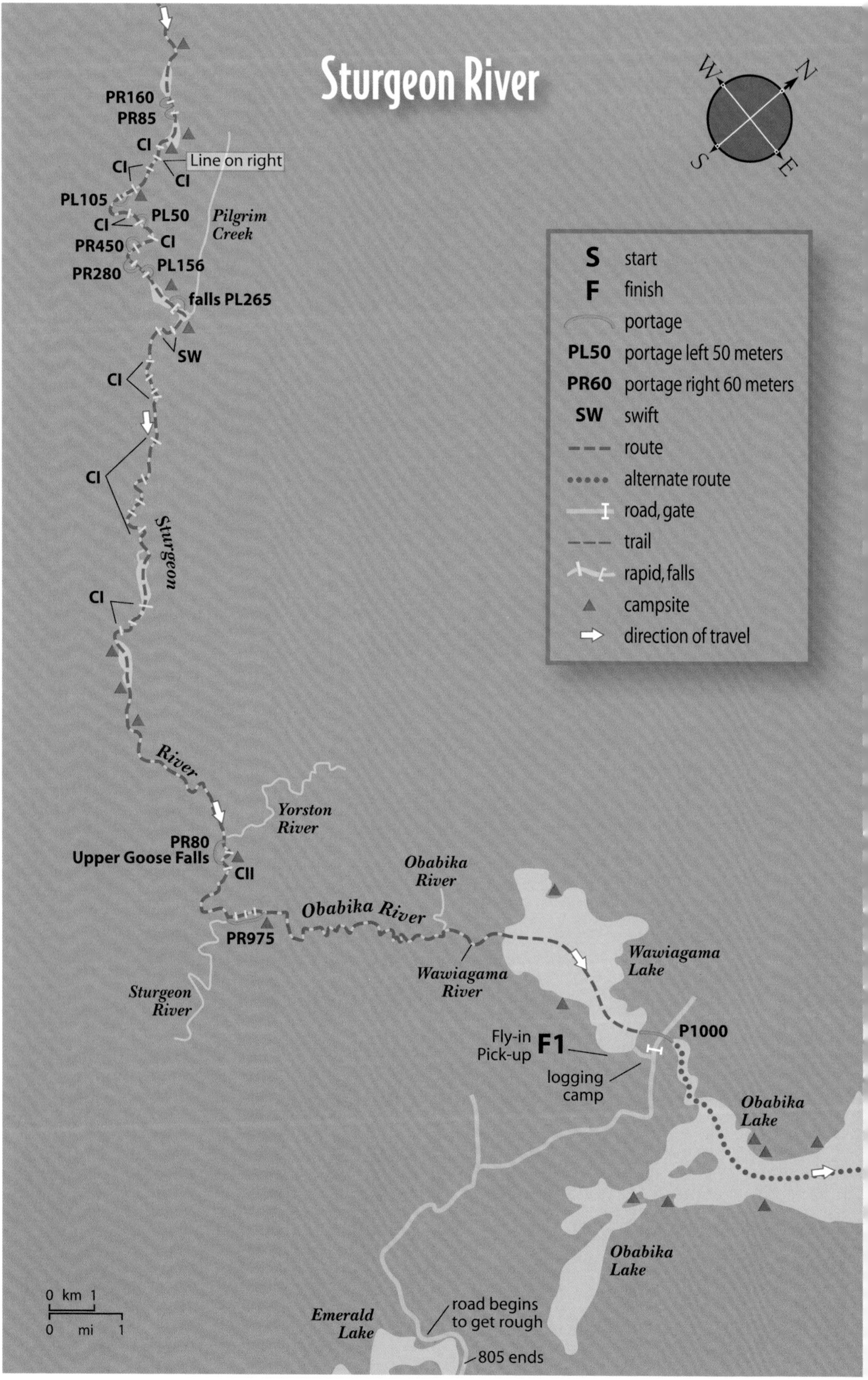

Sturgeon River

PR160
PR85
CI
CI — Line on right
CI
PL105 **PL50** *Pilgrim Creek*
CI **CI**
PR450
PR280 **PL156**
falls PL265
SW
CI
CI
CI
Sturgeon
River

S	start
F	finish
	portage
PL50	portage left 50 meters
PR60	portage right 60 meters
SW	swift
– – –	route
•••••	alternate route
	road, gate
– –	trail
	rapid, falls
▲	campsite
⇨	direction of travel

Yorston River

PR80
Upper Goose Falls **CII**

Obabika River

PR975

Obabika River

Sturgeon River

Wawiagama River

Wawiagama Lake

Fly-in
Pick-up **F1**
logging camp

P1000

Obabika Lake

Obabika Lake

Emerald Lake

road begins
to get rough

805 ends

0 km 1
0 mi 1

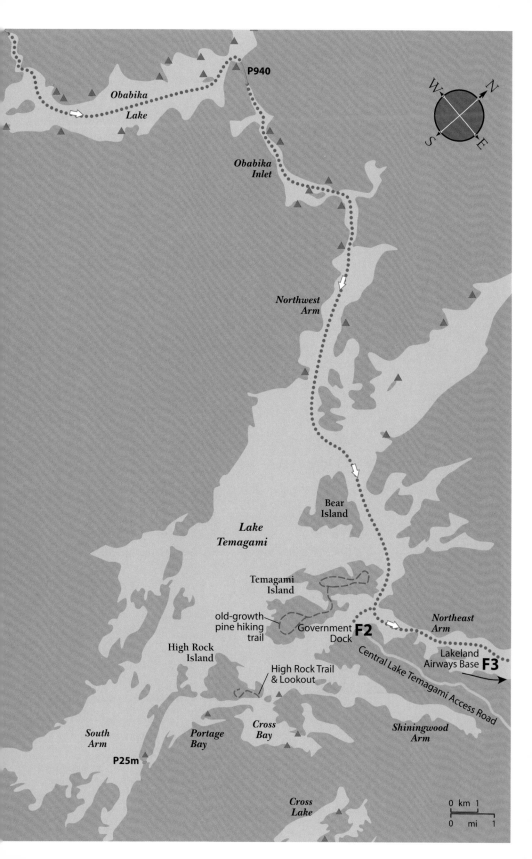

from shore. Both can be portaged, the first by way of a 140-yard (130 m) trail on the left and the second by way of a 104-yard (95 m) trail on the right.

Midway down the third-last rapid I spotted my first bear of the season. I was rather preoccupied with what was ahead of me and didn't manage to see the bruin until he slid down from a thin black spruce only a paddle's-length away. The brief encounter was part frightening and part comic relief. While gawking up at the bear, I somehow hit the only rock in the rapid and lodged myself against it. In the meantime, the bear fell into the river butt first, shook its fur like a wet dog and then retreated into the woods.

The Kettle Falls portage is insane. It is only 377 yards (345 m) long, but you have to be half mountain goat to survive it. First you have to climb almost straight up from the take-out (marked to the right), then wander aimlessly up on top in search of the correct trail that will eventually lead down an even steeper slope to reach the put-in. It was arduous work for me. The only advantage was that after tripping twice and then having the canoe come crashing down on my head, I was finally forced to slow down and concentrate on what I was doing.

Four more portages are necessary directly after Kettle Falls. The first (209 yards [190 m]) is marked to the left of the pond just below the falls; the second and third (115 yards and 142 yards [105 m, 130 m]) are both marked on the right and avoid a double set of rapids between Renfrew Lake and Perkins Lake. The fourth (292 yards [265 m]) is to the far right of the rapid, at the southernmost end of Perkins Lake.

I used the first, third and fourth portage but managed to run the second rapid, though completely by accident, of course. The rapid was made up of two chutes. I ran the first one intentionally and then the second unintentionally. In hindsight, I know I took too long to figure out my next move after the first drop. Just as I was attempting to eddy into the right, the current grabbed hold of my boat and sent me down the second chute backward. It was an absolute miracle that I stayed upright all the way to the bottom. If not, I would have been swept down the third rapid, which just happened to be a small falls.

The rapids continue, with two shallow sections before Hazel Lake and three more swifts at the outlet, followed shortly after by three more rapids just before an extended pond (only the first requires a 110-yard [100 m]) portage on the right).

By the time I reached the south end of the pond, the skies had begun to cloud up. So I portaged 170 yards (160 m) to the right of a large chute as well as 94 yards (85 m) to the right of an extreme technical rapid, swept down four somewhat easy Class Is, and then made haste down a Class II to set up a dry camp midway along a 115-yard (105 m) portage to the left — just before the downpour began.

The rain had tapered off by morning and I was back on the river early, taking on three Class I rapids (the second has a 55-yard [50 m]) portage on the left) before entering a small pond.

Then, after running down a small swift, I took on two extremely rugged portages (490 yards and 306 yards [450 m, 280 m], both marked to the right) to

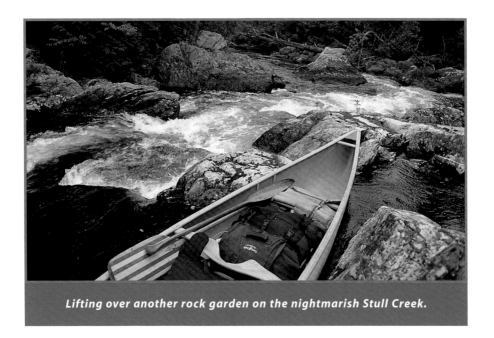
Lifting over another rock garden on the nightmarish Stull Creek.

avoid two major drops. The put-in of the second portage was so steep I was forced to tie a rope to the stern of the canoe and then lower it down to the water.

Next is a technical Class I rapid with an optional 171-yard (156 m) portage to the left, followed soon after by a stunted falls with a mandatory 292-yard (265 m) portage also on the left. Then, where jack pine flats and gravel bars begin to dominate the landscape, over a dozen shallow rapids make for exceptional paddling. There's only an 88-yard (80 m) portage to the right of Upper Goose Falls, situated not far downstream from the confluence of the Yorston and Sturgeon Rivers, to force you out of your canoe.

I should have stopped to make camp on a prime site on the east side of Upper Goose Falls, but my nervousness was still causing me to hurry along. I ended up convincing myself that the site at the end of the Obabika River portage would be a better place to end the day. So I ran down the Class II rapid below the falls and twenty minutes later pulled up on a gravel bank just downstream, where the Obabika empties into the Sturgeon.

It took me another twenty minutes to walk to the end of the 1,073-yard (975 m) trail, only to find a makeshift site infested with mosquitoes and black-flies. Of course, rather than slap on the bug juice and make the best of things, I continued on up the Obabika, thinking that I could actually reach Wawiagama Lake well before nightfall.

What a mistake! The current on the Obabika was surprisingly strong and the silty bottom made poling up river impossible. Four hours later, after lifting over half-a-dozen logjams and paddling up a dead-end creek I mistook for the route into Wawiagama Lake, the light was beginning to fade and thunderheads grumbled overhead. In vain I searched the shoreline for any patch of rock or a mild slope to camp on, but not a single spot presented itself.

I guess I should have paid more attention to a 1905 description of the same route that I happened to pick up at the local library before my trip. It was written by four men from Ohio (aided by five Native guides, including Frank Commanda) who, after tracking up the Sturgeon as far as Kettle Falls, turned tail and ascended the Obabika. They described the upstream paddle as "Two miles of the hardest kind of paddle exercise against a vicious current that sapped the strength from their ancient arms."

I was just thinking about turning back and walking out on a newly constructed logging bridge I had passed under some ways downstream when, on the right bank, I noticed a faded orange ribbon dangling from an alder branch. Below it was a soft current of silt-free water. I pushed aside some brush, and there it was — the "mighty" Wawiagama River. It was like opening up the gateway to a lost world.

The narrow waterway had far more curves in it than the Obabika, and was blocked with even more logjam, but at least I knew where I was. In fact, I actually started to enjoy the challenge of making my way upstream. Forty minutes later I rounded the last bend, lifted over one more pile of logs, and paddled out into the expanse of Wawiagama Lake.

By now the sun was beginning to set, its light spectacular, streaming through the dark storm clouds coming in from the west. A quick glance at the map revealed a designated site about halfway along the south shore. The storm was only minutes away, though, and rather than risk being caught out in the rain, I pulled up on the first flat spot I came to. My canoe-tripping ethics say this method of camping isn't proper, but I couldn't see how staying for one night would result in much wear and tear on the wilderness.

The rain began the moment I reached shore. I quickly erected a tarp and foraged enough wood for a small fire, just enough to heat water for tea and create a bit of smoke to chase away bugs. The fire was built directly under the tarp, atop bare granite, and I plucked a few rocks from the lake to circle the flames. Then, as I waited for the water to boil, I pulled out my sleeping bag from my pack and crawled in. Before the water even began to sizzle, however, I fell deep asleep, finally feeling at peace with my surroundings.

Temagami's Sturgeon River

TIME 5 to 7 days	**LONGEST PORTAGE** 1,073 yards (975 m)
PORTAGES 19 (not including route choice from Hamlow Lake to Sturgeon River)	**BEST TIME TO RUN IT** Early to late spring

FEE There's the moderate cost for the flight into Scarecrow, but the Sturgeon is an unmaintained provincial park and no camping permit is required.

ALTERNATIVE ROUTE It's easier on your vehicle to meet Lakeland Airways at the home base in Temagami and then return by way of a 1,100-yard (1,000 m) portage from Wawiagama Lake to Obabika and then a 1,028-yard (940 m) portage from Obabika to Lake Temagami. You can also cut the strenuous trip from Hamlow Lake to the Sturgeon River by having the pilot drop you off at Paul Lake.

OUTFITTERS

Lakeland Airways
Box 249
Temagami, Ontario
P0H 2H0
705-569-3455
www.lakelandthreebuoys.com

Wanapitei Canoe Inc.
Sandy Inlet
Temagami, Ontario
P0H 2H0
705-237-8677
(Summer)
338 Caves Road
R.R. 2
Warsaw, Ontario
K0L 3A0
1-888-781-0411
705-652-9461
(Winter)
www.wanapiteicanoe.com

Smoothwater Outdoor Center
Box 40
Temagami, Ontario
P0H 2H0
705-569-3539
www.smoothwater.com

**Temagami Wilderness
  Center Limited**
RR 1
Temagami, Ontario
P0H 2H0
705-569-3733
www.temagami.com

Temagami Outfitting Company
Box 512, 20 Lakeshore Drive
Temagami, Ontario
P0H 2H0
705-569-2595
www.icanoe.ca

FOR MORE INFORMATION
Ministry of Natural Resources
3301 Trout Lake Road
North Bay, Ontario
P1A 4L7
705-475-5550

MAPS The Ministry of Natural Resources has produced a canoe map for the Temagami District. Hap Wilson's guidebook, *Temagami Canoe Routes*, is also an excellent resource.

TOPOGRAPHIC MAPS
4 P/7, 41 P/2, 41 I/15, 41 I/16 & 41 I/9
Provincial Series: Scale 1:100,000
Maple Mountain 41 P/SE & Capreol
41 I/NE

The West Montreal River

I HAD VISITED THE MONTREAL RIVER TWICE BEFORE, once as a teenager, on a father-and-son fishing trip, and then again just after college while working for the Ministry of Natural Resources as a tree planter. This time I would travel the river alone by canoe, taking time out to revisit the trees that I had put to root, and then to share in another fishing trip with my father. And somewhere along the way I would gain a clear perspective on the time I had wasted planting trees for the government and the time I took for granted fishing with my father.

My retrospective journey began just a few miles west of Gowganda, at the Edith Lake access point. (Take the Edith Lake road for a little more than a mile (2 km) north of Highway 560.) The night before I stayed at Auld Reekie Lodge, located on the south side of the highway and just west of the Edith Lake road, and left the lodge owner a spare key to my truck so he could shuttle it down to the take-out at Wapus Creek. Parking is available at a roadside picnic site on the north side of Highway 560, 10 miles (16 km) west of Gowganda.

It wasn't long after shoving off from the boat launch at Edith Lake that I came to the first portage en route, measuring 165 yards (150 m) and marked to the right of a small falls. (There's a choice of two take-outs.)

A number of boats were stored at the end of the trail. By the looks of them, they were the same ones that my father and I had to choose from when we fished here more than twenty years before. At first, this was where we had planned our reunion, fishing the expanse of Obushkong Lake to the north. But we remembered how little we caught back then, and chose instead to rendezvous at a lodge halfway along Mistinikon Lake — about a three-to-four-day paddle from this point.

For old times' sake though, I did throw my line in and trolled up the entire length of the lake. When I reached the marshy north end, where the river turns dramatically to the right, I hooked onto a miniature perch — obviously nothing here had changed.

The weedy channel continued to make navigation difficult up until East Beaver Lake. Here the river heads northward again, squeezing through a group of rocky islands capped with a stand of jack pine. It was a great spot to stop for lunch, so I gave the canoe one last stroke, and let the bow slice into the sandy shoreline. Before unpacking my food bag, however, I decide to take a swim. The island was secluded; actually the entire lake reeked with solitude, and I was unlikely to have anyone surprise me in my birthday suit. But being a tad modest, I took one last look across the water before I removed my clothes.

I wasn't always paranoid about skinny-dipping. It started a few years back when I was caught fully exposed out on a rock ledge in Killarney Provincial Park. For six days I had been alone (which was unusual for such a busy park), and I decided to swim naked in the cool water of Nellie Lake. Then, while submerged, I heard, or actually felt, a rumble across the water. I came back up to the surface to witness a water bomber taking a load of water from the center of the lake.

Worried that a forest fire might actually be nearby, I quickly swam for shore, climbed up the nearest outcrop of rock, and then looked out over the horizon for any sign of smoke. That's when I got caught. Some girls' camp from Sudbury paddled by and spotted me totally naked up on the rock. They giggled. Embarrassed as hell, I started to run full-tilt back down toward my canoe. On the way down, however, I managed to trip on an exposed root, and rolled most of the way, cutting my knee wide open. The leader, an attractive twenty-something blonde, asked if I needed first aid. I stuttered out, "No thanks, I'm fine," and the group paddled on, laughing uncontrollably as they made their way across the lake.

After my short break on East Beaver Lake, I continued on just west of the river outlet and began portaging to the left of a giant logjam. The 266-yard

Red Pine Narrows.

(243 m) trail, which leads to the south end of Crotch Lake, had hardly been used. In fact, it actually disappeared on me just after a small chute. So rather than push myself through the brush, I foolishly jumped back into the canoe and paddled on. Of course, the rapids were far from over. As I rounded the next bend, I came face to face with a wall of huge standing waves. I quickly anchored myself by grabbing hold of an alder bush. Then, hanging on to the lining ropes attached to the bow and stern, I leaped out of the canoe and began walking it down like a dog on a leash.

Everything was going great until, in a brief second, the stern leaned a little too far downstream. The current immediately took full advantage of the situation and sucked the canoe under, yanking me into the water at the same time. Instantly I released both ropes and allowed the boat, my gear, and myself to be flushed down the whitewater that remained.

At the next rapid, found soon after you enter the eastern outlet, I made sure to finish the entire 443-yard (405 m) portage (marked to the right of a log dam) before heading off again. Not far from the put-in, however, I did manage to run a long and challenging set of rapids without mishap. (There is a 545-yard [495 m] path on the right of the last and most difficult set.)

Just over half a mile (1 km) downstream from the last rapid is Split Falls. At first I considered making an early camp on the site between the two drops. But after I noticed a pile of trash left behind by the previous users, I paddled over to the right and took the 130-yard (120 m) portage into Tommy Lake.

The two sites on Tommy Lake were also littered with pop cans and fishing line, however, so I continued even further. First, I portaged 160 yards (145 m) to the left of another falls, then, after entering a small pond by way of a quick swift, I ran down an easy Class I rapid and finally made camp on an island close to Sisseney Lake's western shore.

Sisseney Lake is gorgeous — made up of gravel beaches, groves of birch and a scattering of red and white pine — and I wish I could have spent some time fishing its shoreline that evening. The bugs were so brutal, however, that I found myself fleeing to the tent well before dusk. The entire night I heard the buzzing of mosquitoes through the thin wall of nylon and only dared to venture out twice; once to pee and the other time to stop a beaver from gnawing a nearby poplar down on me.

I tried to cook breakfast the next morning while wrapped up in a one-piece bug-suit, but soon resorted to eating on the run, munching on plain granola as I paddled to the far north end of Sisseney Lake. Here, a 330-yard (300 m) portage was marked to the left of a double set of rapids. But I had no desire to head back to the bug-infested shore. So, after going slowly over the first drop — dodging some steel pegs sticking out from the remains of an old log chute — I continued on down the second rapid without any difficulty.

The fun continued about a mile (1.5 km) downriver. Here, I ran a quick and easy swift (a 66-yard [60 m] portage is on the left), passed under a hydro line, and then went down an incredibly long series of Class I rapids (a long but flat 836-yard [765 m] portage cuts through the bush on the left).

Because I'd avoided having to portage, it was only midmorning when I reached the forks of the Montreal. This is the spot where the main river bends southeast toward the town of Elk Lake and the West Montreal comes down from Matachewan. Most canoeists obviously go with the current, but when paddling this route a few years back, I found the landscape quite dull, as it passes mostly through the district's clay belt area. So this time, even though it meant paddling upstream for the rest of the way, I decided to give the west branch a try.

In the town of Matachewan, only a half-hour paddle up from the forks, a small swift under the highway bridge forced me to carry my gear around to the right. I took out at a municipal park, crossed the highway, and then headed back down to the river just left of an abandoned gas station. But rather than continue on, I thought I'd take advantage of a nearby tavern and treat myself to brunch.

As I approached the entrance to the hotel, I caught a glimpse of two dead bears (victims of the spring bear hunt) hung upside down from a metal pole. Inside, stuffed animals adorned the walls. A sign posted over the bar read No Hunting or Fishing Knifes Allowed. And a group of hunters, dressed in full fatigues, sat in the corner discussing their recent kill over cigarettes and coffee.

When I walked in and claimed a table near the bar, everyone seemed to turn and stare. I was definitely out of place, wearing Teva sandals, bright Patagonia quick-dry shorts, and a T-shirt with a cartoon depiction of a canoeist harpooning a Sea-doo. I think if I were wearing a Tilley hat my chances of survival would have been slim at best.

I sat down and ordered coffee. A man in a red flannel shirt turned round at the bar and eyed me. "Ya do know you're going the wrong way, eh?"

"Pardon?" I replied, trying to control a jittery twitch.

"Well, most canoeists go downriver, ya know," he answered, and then walked over to sit across from me, introducing himself as Rick.

Incredibly nervous at this point, I rambled off an elongated explanation, telling everyone in the tavern about wanting to visit the trees I had planted near here fourteen years ago and then meet my father for a fishing trip just upriver. And then, whether it was because I gave evidence that I was a fellow angler or the simple fact that I had once worked in the neighboring bush, everyone seemed to treat me differently. Rick even poured me a second cup of coffee and then offered to drive me to where he thought I might have planted the trees.

I was a little wary at first (visions of the movie *Deliverance* danced through my head), but Rick seemed like a decent guy. Besides, I really wanted to see those trees. So I took up his offer and ordered a bacon sandwich to go.

Rick drove for a good twenty minutes before turning off a backroad. It wasn't long after, though, when I spotted the plantation up on a rise. It was

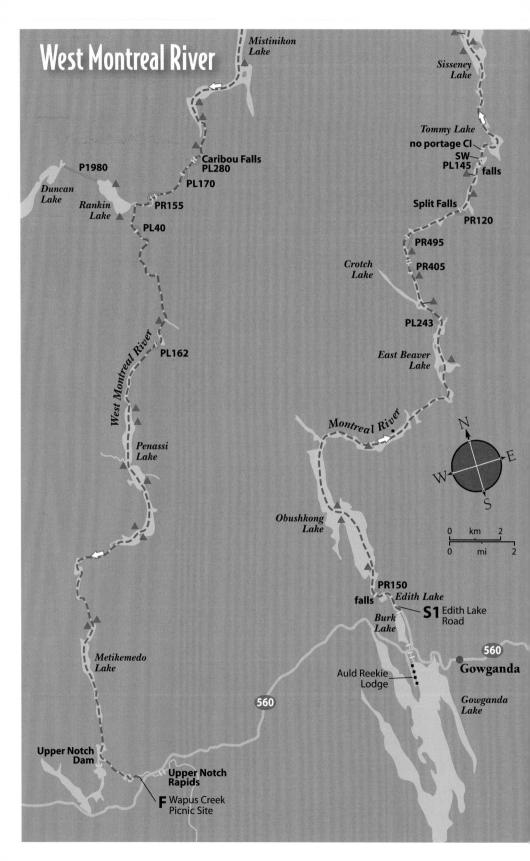

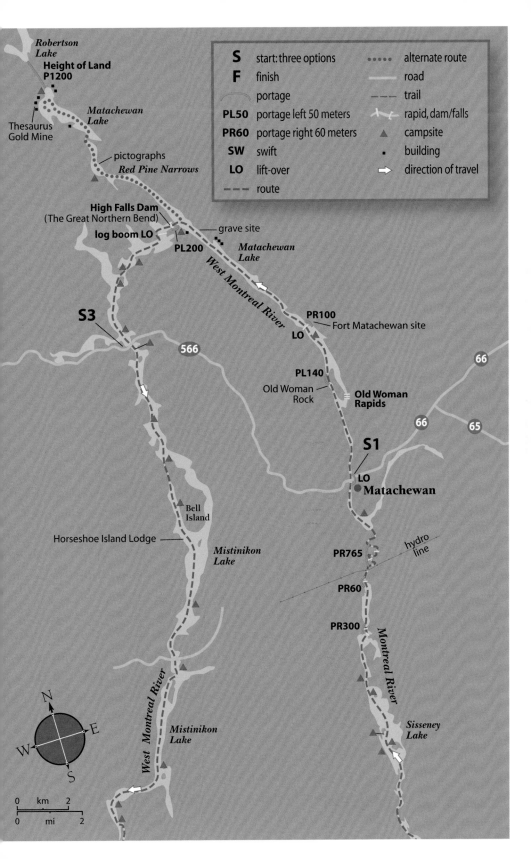

surrounded by a massive clear-cut, however, and looked more like a row of corn ready to be harvested than a future forest.

I was surprised at my anger. After cutting timber for two winters in the mid-1980s, I thought I'd gained a wide tolerance for woodsmen and what they do. But I guess what really upset me was the sign posted beside the stale environment I had created: Proposed Cut 1999. I was reminded then that during my career as a forest technician I was never a manager of forest ecology. I was just a damn farmer.

I didn't want to discuss the issue with Rick. He was a true northerner, a man who chose to live in a resource-dependent community, and to him I was just some canoeist from the south passing through. So I thanked him for the tour and made small talk all the way back into town.

It was noon by the time I was paddling north again, reaching Old Woman Rapids, about 2 miles (3 km) upstream from Matachewan. The portage itself is nowhere near the rapids. Instead, I paddled up the long inlet to the left and found a mine track heading up and over a rise. Sitting at the take-out was a cart connected to a motorized winch installed at the crest of the hill, but I kept to tradition and carried my canoe over the 153 yards (140 m). On my way back to retrieve my pack, I remembered Rick telling me about the "Old Woman" — the profile of a face formed in the rock on the west side of the river — and I caught a glimpse of her silhouette while heading back down the hill. (Look to where someone has recently cleared the trees in front of the rock face.)

The next obstacle on the way was a set of rapids beside the site of Fort Matachewan — once an important supply depot for the entire area between 1865 and 1920. Here you can either use a 55-yard (50 m) lift-over on the left or a 110-yard (100 m) bush trail on the right. I chose the right in hopes of spotting some small fragments of the historic fort, but only a few rotten timbers were strewn about in the bush and a tangle of dogwood and alder made it impossible to explore any further inland. I later found out that most of the buildings — including a storehouse and a church with a cemetery — were much further back from the river, partway up a hill. (In the cemetery is the grave of Stephen Lafrician, the last caretaker of the fort, who had the American Veterans Association provide him with a tombstone for his services during the Civil War.)

Almost 4 miles (6 km) upriver, after the Montreal passes a line of steel towers placed here by the Great Northern Power Company in 1924, I approached what's known as the Great Northern Bend. This is where a 46-foot (14 m) cascade called High Falls joins the west branch of the river with the east branch, and where the route itself makes an abrupt turn to the south.

Almost directly across High Falls was a row of cabins, one of which happened to be occupied by six over-enthusiastic fishermen from Ohio. As soon as they saw me canoe by, I was invited in for a beer. I quickly took up their offer — how could I resist? Then I agreed to several more after that, and found myself spending the night crashed out on their spare bunk.

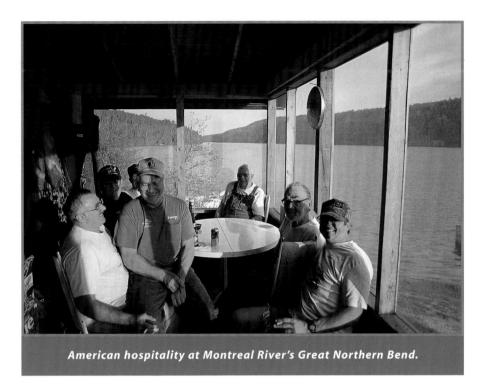

American hospitality at Montreal River's Great Northern Bend.

I was late getting started the following morning (maybe a tad hung over), so rather than turning at the "bend" in the river, I decided to continue north, up what's known as the "backwater" of High Falls. My new plan was to make camp for my third night on the north shore of Matachewan Lake. The route was totally out of my way. What inspired me were stories of lost gold mines, hidden graves, historic portages, and ancient rock paintings — stories told to me by George, the oldest of the Ohio fishermen, who had been coming up here for thirty-six years.

First on George's list was the grave of a woodcutter named Joe Metote. He drowned during the construction of the High Falls Dam in 1927, and was found three years later and buried almost directly across from the falls, about 33 yards (30 m) up in the bush. All that remained now was a broken-down cedar fence and a wooden marker with Joe's name worn almost completely off.

Then, not far past Red Pine Narrows and slightly to the east, was a rock decorated with Indian pictographs (a shaman boat, heron prints and some type of lizard). I had no tobacco with me, so I left an offering of GORP (I figured the spirits would appreciate it since it was the last of my supply), and then continued on through another narrows to make camp beside an old log cabin on the north end of Matachewan Lake.

The spot wasn't really a true campsite, just a small clearing along the shore, and I guess the designated site I saw earlier across from the rock paintings would have been a better choice.

But I wanted to stay closer to Matachewan Lake's northeastern end where George had marked on my map the whereabouts of the great Thesaurus gold rush (started by James Chester Nelson in 1918) as well as the height-of-land portage once used by the residents of Fort Matachewan to reach James Bay.

Eight claims were supposedly worked here and a number of housekeeping cabins were reported to be along the shoreline and even more working shanties about a twenty-minute walk back in the bush. I didn't find much of anything, however. But I did manage to locate the old blaze marking the height-of-land portage, and I carried the 1,320 yards (1,200 m) into Robertson Lake (stay to the right after the fork) and spent the entire afternoon catching a mess of pike.

Day four was when I planned to meet my father at Horseshoe Island Lodge, halfway along Mistinikon Lake. So I was up early, made a quick visit to my American friends who were fishing at the base of High Falls, and then headed over to use the 220-yard (200 m) portage to the left of the dam. A log cabin (owned by Bill McDonell between 1926 and 1954, when he controlled the dam) is to the left of the take-out. From here the trail headed up a sandy hill, and then to the right and alongside the falls.

Around the corner from the put-in, after lifting over to the left of a log boom, I headed out along Mistinikon Lake's eastern outlet. By keeping to the left I then managed to find my way through a cluster of small islands and to where the main body of the lake heads directly south.

Mistinikon was a long haul. Once past the Highway 566 bridge, the lake grew busy with cottagers and fishermen darting back and forth in their aluminum boats. The shoreline remained mostly wild, however, and offered a number of prime rock outcrops where I could get out and stretch my legs. The prevailing winds also helped me along, and by midafternoon I had reached Bell Island, the centerpiece of Mistinikon Lake. I kept to the west of the island and not long after, caught a glimpse of my father and his fishing companion, John Addison, jigging for walleye just out from the lodge.

Immediately I yelled out, "How's the fishing this year?" And laughed when I heard my father's reply: "Same as the last time. Lousy!"

It was a short visit, lasting only three days, but we shared plenty of boat time, fishing time and river time. In fact, except that our trip twenty years ago lasted five days, things were quite the same. And other than giving out excuses on why the fish weren't biting and teasing the heck out of poor John because he was too afraid to bait his own hook with a leech, we made little conversation — and did little thinking, for that matter, about how our times shared together out in the wilds helped mature our relationship. It was just one of those things we did, I guess, one of those fun trips that father and sons don't think too much about until long after they're over.

I still had 22 miles (36 km) of paddling to do after my stay at Horseshoe Lodge, and only two days to do it in. The first day was spent crossing what remained of Mistinikon Lake and then portaging 306 yards (280 m) around the left of Caribou Falls. Then, before making camp on the northwest shore of

Rankin Lake, I completed two more portages — a 186 yard (170 m) to the left and a 170 yard (155 m) to the right. (In low water levels, it's probably best to line or wade up the two rapids.)

The upstream battle continued on the second and final day. I had to deal with only two more sets of shallow rapids, however. The first had a 44-yard (40 m) portage on the left and the second had a 177-yard (162 m) portage, also on the left. Then a simple paddle across Penassi and Metikemedo Lakes, followed by a quick turn to the left at the forks not far from the Wapus Creek take-out point along Highway 560, was all that was left of my journey back in time.

The West Montreal River

TIME 5 to 7 days

DIFFICULTY The route is rated for novice paddlers with moderate canoe-tripping skills, but it is no longer being properly maintained by the Ministry of Natural Resources.

PORTAGES 16

LONGEST PORTAGE
836 yards (765 m)

BEST TIME TO RUN IT
Spring through fall

FEE The route travels through Crown land, where no fee is required for Canadian citizens. A small fee is charged for the shuttle.

ALTERNATIVE ROUTE The route can be cut short by either beginning or ending at the town of Matchewan. You can also complete a five-day loop back to Gowganda by using the East Branch of the Montreal and Sydney Creek.

OUTFITTERS
Auld Reekie Lodge
General Delivery
Gowganada, Ontario
P0J 1J0
705-624-3512
www.virtualnorth.com/auldreekie/

FOR MORE INFORMATION
Ministry of Natural Resources
Kirkland Lake
Box 910
10 Government Road East
P2N 3K4
705-568-3222

MAPS The Ministry of Natural Resources has produced a pamphlet titled *Gowganda to Matachewan Routes*. Hap Wilson's guidebook, *Temagami Canoe Routes*, is also an excellent resource.

TOPOGRAPHIC MAPS
41 P/10, 41 P/15, 42 A/2 & 41 P/16
Provincial Series: Scale 1:100,000
Elk Lake 41 P/NE & Kirkland Lake
42 A/SE

Bardney Lake, Mississagi River.

The Mississagi River
Land of Grey Owl

MY WIFE, ALANA, AND I HAVE ALWAYS WANTED TO PADDLE the Mississagi River. What kept us from organizing a trip, however, was the reality of the lengthy car shuttle needed to travel the best portion, between Biscotasing and Aubrey Falls — most of this 110-mile (177 km) stretch being under the protection of a Provincial Waterway Park. Then, while browsing the shelves of a used bookstore, I happened upon a copy of Grey Owl's *Tales of an Empty Cabin*, which includes a detailed description of canoeing the Mississagi.

"For this is no ordinary stream, but a very King among rivers . . . the Grand Discharge of Waters of the Indians, pouring its furious way between rockbound shores, sweeping a path for twice a hundred miles through forest lands, levying tribute, in all its branches, from four thousand square miles of territory, untamed, defiant and relentless, arrogantly imposing its name on all surrounding country; so that a man may travel many a day by canoe and portage through an intricate network of stream and lake and forest, among a rich infinite variety of scenery and still be within Mississagi's far-flung principality . . ."

How can any canoeists read such an elaborate account and not want to see it for themselves? In a week, my wife and I were packed and driving north to the Mississagi.

To deal with the long two-and-a-half-hour car shuttle, Alana and I had Missinaibi Headwaters (summer, 705-444-7804 or 1-800-590-7836; winter, 705-444-7780) meet us at the parking lot for the Aubrey Falls Hiking Trail, which is marked by a provincial park sign on the right side of Highway 129, 67 miles (108 km) north of Thessalon. We left our vehicle behind and allowed the outfitters to drive us to the access point. It would have been cheaper to have a local outfitter drive up to the access point with us and then shuttle our truck back to the parking lot, but with most of the drive being on a gravel logging road, it seemed a better choice to have Missinaibi Headwaters worry about the wear and tear on their own vehicle.

From the parking lot we headed north on Highway 129 for a good hour, and then turned right onto Highway 667. Once past a small hamlet called Sultan, we turned off onto the Sultan Industrial Road (owned by E. B. Eddy) and, rather than driving all the way to Biscotasing, we saved a day of lake paddling by accessing the river just south of Ramsey, putting in at the Spanish Chutes. Take note, however, that the drive along the E. B. Eddy Road is confusing, not to mention dangerous (logging trucks don't take kindly to canoeists hogging their road), and again, it was well worth the money to have Missinaibi Headwaters deal with it all.

From Spanish Chutes the route heads upstream on the Spanish River. The first portage (550 yards [500 m]) is on the left, partway up a small swift. Numerous islands and rock outcrops on Spanish Lake and on Bardney Lake (connected at the southwestern end of Spanish Lake by a 165-yard (150 m) portage to the left of Bardney Creek Dam), make for excellent campsites. Alana and I decided to continue on, though, taking the steep 473-yard (430 m) height-of-land portage to Sulphur Lake before stopping for the day. We signed the register at the put-in, adding to only a dozen other canoeists who had traveled the route before us, and then paddled across to the take-out of the next portage (220 yards [200 m]) to set up camp.

Our first day was an eventful one. By 6:30 p.m. we had dodged insane truck drivers on the 50-mile (80 km) E. B. Eddy Road, hauled ourselves over from one watershed to the next, and then made camp on one of the most remote lakes we had been to in years. Along the way we spotted a total of three bald eagles, a family of curious otters, a solitary moose, the back end of a very shy lynx, and a giant northern pike as it devoured a baby loon only a few yards away from the bow of our canoe. It was obvious to us now that the rich rewards of this isolated river far outweighed the hassles of any lengthy car shuttle.

The next morning was spent paddling a chain of mucky ponds (Surprise Lake and Circle Lake) connected by three portages (a 1,100-yard [1,000 m] trail, cursed with five steep inclines toward the put-in, and two soggy 99-yard [90 m] lift-overs). It was an easy paddle down Mississagi Lake, however, and near the middle of the lake, Alana and I even stepped out of the canoe and onto a sandbar to soak our aching feet — that is, until I noticed a monster leech attached to my big toe.

Mississagi Lake is made up of three sections joined together by a series of shallow narrows. At the south end of the lake, the slow-moving current squeezes its way through another rock-strewn channel that eventually empties out into Upper Green Lake. A modern lodge stands at the entranceway, built in the same location as was the North West Company's post. (The post was constructed in the late 1700s by Montreal traders; the HBC took over the site in 1821.) The fur traders decided on the Upper Green Lake location to accommodate the Natives who had used the river as a travel corridor since prehistoric times. The post was abandoned in 1892, however, when it became easier to ship furs out by rail at Biscotasing.

The route heads southeast now, across a large bay. There's a fire tower on the left-hand shore, perched high above a stand of stout pine. Alana and I went to stop for lunch where the trail heads up to the tower and came across our first group of canoeists — a youth camp from Algonquin who make this spot an annual pilgrimage. They invited us to join them in climbing the tower but we immediately declined, claiming that we had to be on our way before the wind picked up out on the lake. High winds are a problem on Upper Green Lake. In a fact, well-known artist and canoeists Tom Thomson and friend W. S. Broadhead, out on a two-month sketching trip down the Mississagi River, swamped their canoe here during a thunderstorm. But the danger of heavy winds seemed a poor excuse for Alana and me, since there wasn't even a slight breeze blowing across the lake. The truth of the matter was that we were both squeamish about scrambling up a dilapidated fire tower in the middle of nowhere with a group of over-enthusiastic youths.

The portage connecting the southeast bay of Upper Green Lake and Kashbogama Lake is an easy 99 yards (90 m), marked to the left of a short rapid (look for the old telegraph wire embedded in the giant pine near the put-in). Shanguish Lake is next, with the 330-yard (300 m) portage beginning at the end of the bay northeast of the rapids themselves. Then a quick 33-yard (30 m) portage to the upper end of Limit Lake soon follows, just before a logging bridge crosses the river. Make sure that you do not follow the road here. The trail is directly to the left of the rapid.

Alana and I ended our second day on Limit Lake. We first looked for a site on the north end, but the two designated sites were littered with empty beer bottles (the offenders must have come in on the logging road). So we continued down the lake, lost more than once trying to find the way to the southwest bay, and then set up camp on the island just before the 66-yard (60 m) portage leading into Kettle Lake. It was a typical bush site, furnished with a makeshift fire-ring, a table made from pieces of driftwood, and a wooden tent frame under which Alana pitched our own tent. We cooked our diner on a slab of rock on the island's north end where the wind was stronger and the bugs were less fierce. The feast consisted of pita bread and tabbouli mixed in a hot spicy salsa sauce, washed down with white wine.

In the morning we had our coffee and pancakes on the same slab of rock, enjoying the warming air. Then we carried over to Kettle Lake. We kept to the right shore, staying between the large island and the shore until we met up with the river once again to the southwest. To enter Upper Bark Lake we first made use of two quick, 66-yard (60 m) portages to avoid a double set of rapids; the first is marked to the right and the second to the left, at the end of a small bay directly across from first portage. Not far downstream the river twists to the right and eventually empties out into Upper Bark Lake.

We now headed southwest until the river curved to the left. There, it flushes down a shallow swift and then out into the lower section of Upper Bark Lake. The regular route continues east from here and then eventually snakes its way back to the west. It's a scenic tour of Bark Lake — what Grey Owl describes as "a large body of water, beautiful with its islands, inlets and broken, heavily timbered shores." The paddle takes up most of the day, however, and most canoeists make use of a shortcut by continuing southwest down a shallow narrows (the entrance marked by a dilapidated beaver dam). A rough 550-yard (500 m) portage leads from there to a small unnamed lake, followed by a 110-yard (100 m) portage to Bark Lake.

At the put-in of the last portage, a group of cabins mark the site of what was the headquarters for the Mississagi Forest Reserve. Grey Owl signed the inside

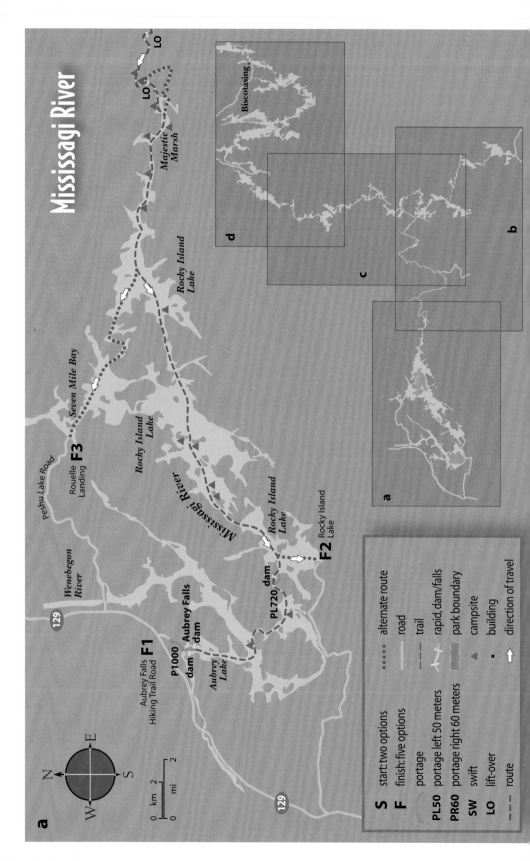

Mississagi River

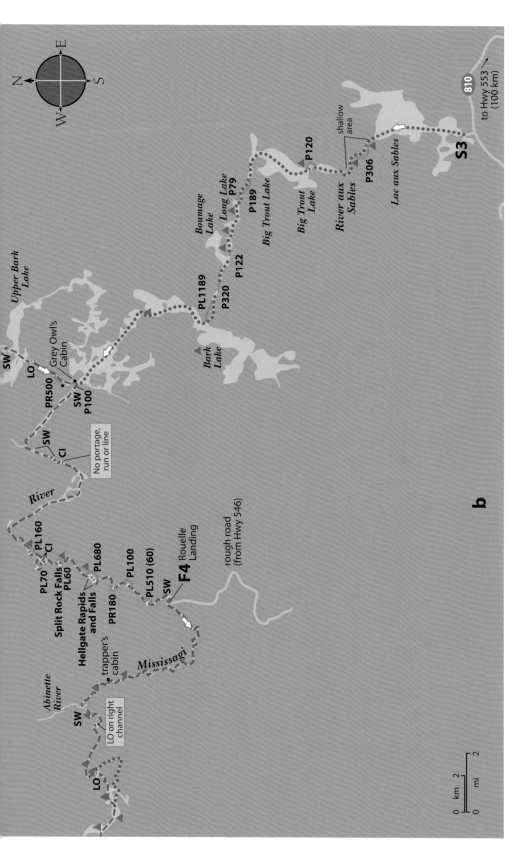

N

W — E

S

Upper Bark
Lake

SW

LO

PR500

Grey Owl's
Cabin

SW
P100

No portage,
run or line

SW

CI

River

SW

PL160

PL70   CI

Split Rock Falls

PL60

Hellgate Rapids
and Falls

PL680

trapper's
cabin

PR180

PL100

PL510 (60)

SW

F4 Rouelle
Landing

rough road
(from Hwy 546)

Mississagi

Abinette
River

SW

LO on right
channel

LO

Bark Lake

PL1189

P320

P122

Boumage
Lake

P189

Long Lake

P79

Big Trout Lake

Big Trout
Lake

River aux
Sables

shallow
area

P306

P120

Lac aux Sables

S3

810

to Hwy 553
(100 km)

b

0   km   2

0   mi   2

Mississagi River

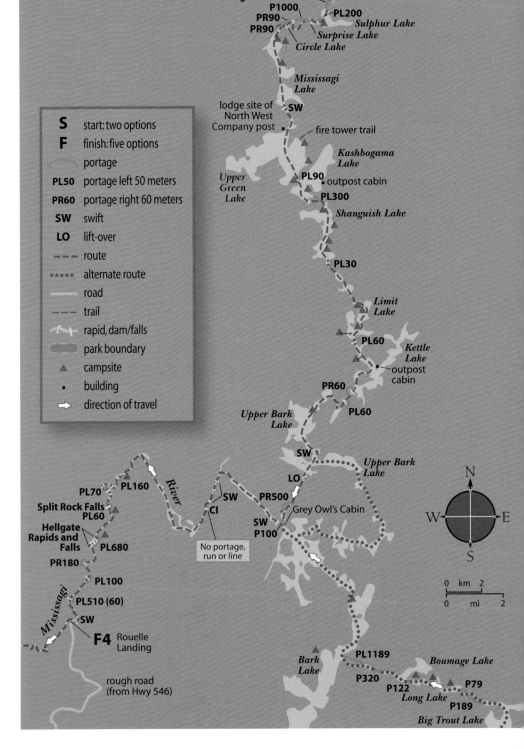

C

S start: two options
F finish: five options
portage
PL50 portage left 50 meters
PR60 portage right 60 meters
SW swift
LO lift-over
--- route
•••• alternate route
road
--- trail
rapid, dam/falls
park boundary
▲ campsite
▪ building
→ direction of travel

Height of Land P430
P1000
PR90 **PL200**
PR90 *Sulphur Lake*
Surprise Lake
Circle Lake

Mississagi Lake

lodge site of
North West   **SW**
Company post ▪   ── fire tower trail

Kashbogama Lake

Upper Green Lake   **PL90**
▪ outpost cabin
PL300
Shanguish Lake

PL30

Limit Lake

PL60
Kettle Lake
▪ outpost cabin

PR60

Upper Bark Lake   **PL60**

SW
Upper Bark Lake

LO

PR500
Grey Owl's Cabin
SW
P100

PL70   **PL160**
Split Rock Falls   *River*
PL60
Hellgate Rapids and Falls   **PL680**
SW
PR180   **CI**

No portage, run or line

PL100

PL510 (60)
SW
F4 Rouelle Landing

rough road
(from Hwy 546)

PL1189   *Boumage Lake*
P320
P122   **P79**
Long Lake   **P189**
Bark Lake   *Big Trout Lake*

N
W ─ E
S

0   km   2
0   mi   2

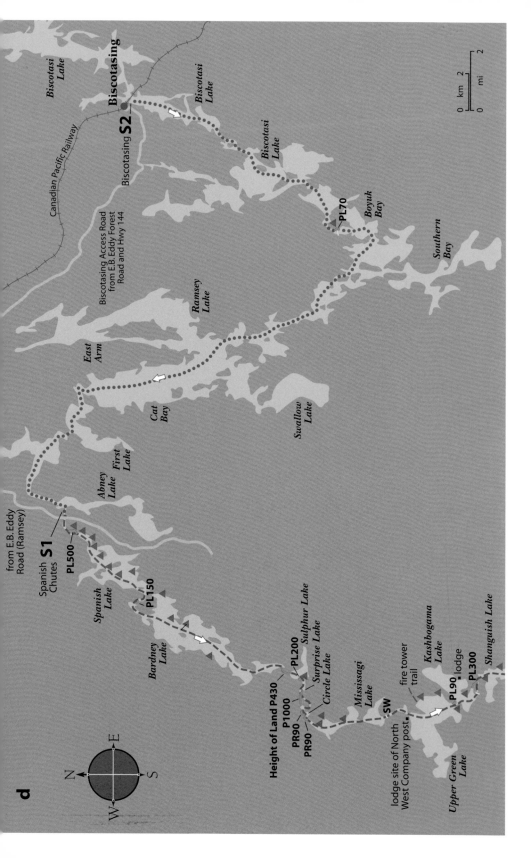

wall of the main log cabin during his stay in 1914, but the cabin is now private and remains locked. On the outside walls, however, other canoeists have left their mark throughout the years: R. Josgauthier (1948), Ray Dickie (1954) and Bisco Ned (1991), to name just a few.

The Mississagi River flows west from here, beginning with a small swift. But it's not until the river twists to the south — about an hour's paddle downstream — that the rapids begin in earnest. Four sets follow in quick succession, all easy runs except maybe the last, which you may want to line your canoe down. The banks then widen out and the river heads northwest, squeezing its way through a cluster of small islands (be sure to stay left to avoid dead-end inlets).

This is where Alana and I should have made camp for our third night out. But we figured the next stretch of fast water, where the river changes course to the southwest again, would provide better campsites, and it was well after 5 p.m. when we reached the next set of rapids. The 175-yard (160 m) portage, marked to the left of the 6-foot drop, had an adequate campsite near the put-in, but a fresh pile of bear dung directly beside the fire ring forced us to continue even further downstream.

It seemed that around every bend in the river there was another rapid — but no campsites. We scouted four main sets and were able to run them all except for the second. Each rapid did come with a short portage (66 to 175 yards [60–160 m]) marked along the left bank.

Then came Split Rock Falls. It was 7:30 p.m. by the time we reached this narrow gorge and, even though the run looked simple enough, we figured it was too late in the day to trust our judgment. So we made use of the 66-yard (60 m) portage to the left and jumped with joy when we found a pristine campsite looking over the scenic drop.

Alana and I slept in the next morning and didn't reach Hellgate Rapids and Falls until mid-morning. The cataract is an incredible spot. After we carried the canoe and packs over the rather strenuous 745-yard (680 m) portage located on the left bank, we backtracked and took the side trail leading to the main drop. Here, while Alana picked a fresh crop of blueberries almost the size of ping-pong balls, I clambered down the moss-covered rocks and snapped half a roll of film.

The strong current remains for at least another two hours downstream, giving you three rapids that require portages (197 yards [180 m] to the right, 110 yards [100 m] to the left, and 558 yards [510 m] also to the left). Take note, however, that the last rapid is made up of three main drops; Alana and I had to carry around the first set only and reduced the 558-yard portage to a mere 66 yards (60 m).

One final swift remains, just before where an access road comes in from Highway 546 (the road is a rough one and is not recommended). Then the river quickly changes character, meandering through a seemingly endless swampy maze interrupted only by clumps of granite topped with stunted spruce and scraggly jack pine. It's a great place for wildlife — moose, otter, osprey and the occasional bald eagle frequent the area — but it's also a breeding ground for mosquitoes and blackflies, and maneuvering your canoe through the constant twists and turns in the river can become irritable work.

After two hours of paddling through the labyrinth, Alana and I met up with a lone trapper who owned the only cabin on this stretch of the river. He had been working on an addition to his cabin for two months and was now taking his powerboat upstream to the Highway 546 access road to meet his wife for a weekend vacation. The man was kind enough, but he had a bad habit of reminding us how quick his boat was compared to our canoe. Once he informed us that it would only take twenty minutes to reach the road (a distance that took us over two hours), Alana, disgruntled, pushed us away with her paddle, wished him and his wife a good holiday, and then silently prayed he would shear a pin while making his way upstream.

Not far from the cabin, just a half hour beyond where the Abinette River empties into the Mississagi, the river forks; to the left is a giant logjam and to the right is a small boulder-strewn rapid. It's possible to portage around the logjam to the left (no trail), but Alana and I found it much easier to lift over and then line down the left side of the small rapid.

Further along, where another massive pile of rotten logs clog the route, the river splits again. The main channel is to the left. Alana and I, however, followed a smaller channel to the right, just past the logjam. We lined to the right of another small rapid, and then snaked our way through a vast field of swamp grass. It was an unplanned shortcut, but we figured the side route saved us over forty minutes of paddling by the time we reached Majestic Marsh — one of the most productive wetland areas in the province.

There are birds by the thousands here: geese, ducks, sandpipers. Where the two channels meet, Alana and I were lucky enough to spot another bald eagle soaring overhead and heard about half-a-dozen sandhill cranes making a ruckus, the sound a lot like a car engine trying to turn over on a cold winter morning. But places to camp are few and far between, with the odd knob of rock providing space for only one or two tents. Having learned our lesson from previous day, however, Alana and I grabbed the first site we came to — a clearing among a patch of spruce. We paddled too far that day. Actually, we had paddled too far every day. So a quick supper was prepared, the tent went up, and we crawled into our sleeping bags well before dusk.

The next morning we were up extra early, eager to reach the expanse of Rocky Island Lake before the wind picked up. The water level was down when we reached the entrance to the lake, revealing hundreds of stumps left behind by the construction of the hydro dams downstream. The shoreline also seemed bare, almost desert-like. It seemed somewhat less than poetic when Alana chanced upon a First Nations crematorium that had been exposed after the water level had reached a record low.

Alana and I had planned to take out below Aubrey Falls, but it is possible to end your trip on Rocky Island Lake by paddling up the north channel, just beyond the large central island, to Seven Mile Bay. The take-out is called Rouelle Landing and is located at the end of the Peshu Lake Road. You can also paddle west to another access road located at the southerly end of the last bay. Both access roads (especially the Peshu Lake Road) can be hard on your vehicle, however, and we figured the extra day spent paddling to Aubrey Falls was worth it.

The morning remained calm and we crossed the middle section of Rocky Island Lake with a great sense of relief. This is a notorious stretch of water where canoeists can easily find themselves windbound for days. Upon reaching the far western narrows, we spotted a colony of tents nestled on top a small island. Other than the mad trapper we had met the day before, this was the first group Alana and I had come across in days, so we gave them a cheerful hello. At first, no one responded. Then a greasy-haired youth stood up and greeted us with his index finger turned up. His buddies laughed, turned up the volume on their boom box and the sweet scent of marijuana smoke drifted toward us. It was obvious that our wilderness experience was quickly coming to an end.

The cluster of islands provided a number of places to camp. But Alana and I decided to give the ruffians a wide berth and took the 788-yard (720 m) portage leading into Aubrey Lake, marked to the left of the hydroelectric dam. We made camp on a small island and, finally feeling somewhat secluded, enjoyed a quick skinny dip from a beach in the back bay.

From our campsite on Aubrey Lake it was only a two-hour paddle to Aubrey Falls. Here, a 1,100-yard (1,000 m) portage, marked between two massive hydro dams, leads back to the parking lot near Highway 129. The portage first heads up a gravel road to the top of the power dam. Then a trail leads down beside the steep slab of concrete, crosses a rocky gorge, and then continues up the opposite side to a viewing area of the falls. It then continues on, over a footbridge and up a gravel path, to the parking lot. Before crossing the footbridge, however, Alana and I took a break to view the 100-foot (30 m) falls. It was impressive, but compared little to what Grey Owl would have witnessed during his travels. Obviously the Mississagi is no longer "untamed, defiant and relentless."

TIME 6 to 8 days

DIFFICULTY Since most of the route is across big lakes, only moderate whitewater skills are needed. The river's remote setting, however, does mean paddlers should have a good level of wilderness tripping skills.

PORTAGES 26

LONGEST PORTAGE
1,100 yards (1,000 m)

BEST TIME TO RUN IT
Spring through fall

FEE Apart from the possible shuttle service, no fee is required.

ALTERNATIVE ROUTE A two day extension can be added from the town of Biscotasing, crossing Biscotasing, Ramsay and First Lake before arriving at the Spanish Chute access. Or, to shorten your trip, you can paddle up from Highway 553 at Lac aux Sables to the south end of Bark Lake by using a series of short portages.

OUTFITTERS
Missinaibi Outfitters
Box 1207
Collingwood, Ontario
L9Y 3Y9
705-444-7804
1-800-590-7836
(off season)

or
Racine Lake
Chapleau, Ontario
P0M 1K0
705-864-2065
(May to September)
www.missinaibi.com

Kegos
R.R. 3
Thessalon, Ontario
P0R 1L0
1-888-698-3889

FOR MORE INFORMATION
Ministry of Natural Resources
190 Cherry Street
Chapleau, Ontario
P0M 1K0
705-864-1710

MAPS The Ministry of Natural Resources has produced a canoe pamphlet titled *Mississagi Canoe Route: Mississagi Provincial Waterway Park.*

TOPOGRAPHIC MAPS
41 0/8, 41 0/1, 41 J/15 & 41 0/2
Provincial Series: Scale 1:100,000
Biscotasing 41 O/SE, Bark Lake 41 J/NE & Wakomata Lake 41 JN/W

The Ivanhoe River

I'LL BE HONEST. The Kinogama/Ivanhoe route has some major drawbacks: the upper stretch of the Kinogama is plagued by countless logjams and shallow water; an unmaintained 3,300-yard (3,000 m) portage marks the entrance to the 22-mile (36 km) Ivanhoe Lake; and there are enough fly-in outpost camps and poorly hidden clear-cuts along the way to eliminate any sense of complete solitude. Still, overall, there are more moose found wandering the portages than canoeists, and the fact that it is a route less traveled far outweighs any of those negatives.

I decided to paddle the route during the last week in May. That doesn't mean that it's a definite spring run, but it was an extremely dry year (1998) and I wanted to take full advantage of any runoff that was left. My partner was Hugh Banks, the Fish and Wildlife Coordinator at Sir Sandford Fleming College in Lindsay (where I lecture part-time). Other instructors had planned to join us but had to bail out when they were called on at the last minute to fight forest fires — ironically, only 31 miles (50 km) east of the canoe route.

Red Pine Lodge, based just off Highway 101 on Ivanhoe Lake, organized our shuttle. It was mid-afternoon when Hugh and I arrived at the lodge and, thinking back, we should have stayed the first night here or at Ivanhoe Provincial Park down the road. But we were both eager to head out on the river, and continued on. At 2 p.m. we drove back out to Highway 101, heading toward Chapleau, then south on Highway 129 until the turnoff for Highway 667. It was a 10.5-mile (17 km) drive to the Kormak bush road (signed to the left) and another 5 miles (8 km) to where a pile of sawdust marks the ghost town of Kormak, named after lumbermen Charles Korpela and Oscar Maki, who began a mill here in 1942. The access point was a small pond directly to the left.

It was close to 4 p.m. by the time we unloaded our gear and handed over the truck keys to our shuttle driver, Gord, so we considered setting up camp directly at the put-in. But then Hugh discovered a pile of rotting meat left behind by hunters for bear bait and so we quickly jumped into our canoe and headed downriver for a safer place to make camp.

Twenty minutes later we still hadn't even reached the railway bridge only 330 yards (300 m) from the access point. We had pulled the canoe over a giant beaver dam, pushed through a wall of cattails and poled through a thick mixture of mud and pond weed. Still desperate to camp far away from the bear bait, we continued down the almost-nonexistent Kinogama River.

The water did eventually open up to the north, into a small lake, but as luck would have it, the river itself twisted eastward, through a thick marsh filled with small logjams and newly constructed beaver dams. Soon the route became impassable and Hugh and I began trying to locate the 550-yard (500 m) portage that our map showed. It would avoid the worst of the logjams by heading up over a hill and into a small lake before rejoining the river.

After a few false starts we finally found the proper take-out, marked to the left by a single piece of blue flagging tape. At first the portage resembled more of a game trail, and we stumbled through the bush trying to keep the faint path in sight. Eventually we came across more blue ribbons, and followed the trail to where it finally came out to an old logging road. There, a bright yellow portage sign marked the portage continuing down a hill to the small unnamed lake. It was obvious that the road was an alternative access point used to avoid the mess we just pushed our way through. After a swift inspection of the road, however, Hugh and I figured having wet sneakers was a far better alternative than ruining the undercarriage of my truck.

It was dark by the time we made camp on the opposite end of the lake. It had to be one of the worst sites I've ever pitched a tent on — at the end of an ATV trail, littered with beer cans, fishing line, used car batteries, dirty diapers and, you guessed it, another pile of rotting meat. But it was too dark to notice the garbage heap and too late to care about the bear bait.

We were back on the river early the next morning, lifting over three more logjams and two more beaver dams before reaching Tooms Lake. Both Hugh and I dragged lures behind the canoe while heading northeast to where the

The confluence of the Kinogama and Ivanhoe Rivers.

Kinogama River flushes out of the lake. Hugh's spinning jig won over my blue Rapala three to one before we reached a bouldery swift formed where a logging bridge once crossed the river. We ran the canoe through and then stopped at the campsite on the left bank for brunch.

From here to Sawbill Lake the river finally opens up and deadfalls become less of a problem. This long stretch is also a haven for wildlife. Even before we reached the halfway point, Hugh and I spotted a wide assortment of ducks, a family of otters, our first of five bald eagles sighted en route, and a cow moose with twin calves. We first noticed the cow. Then the calves showed themselves when we were only about three canoe-lengths away. Mom suddenly bolted, sounded off a muffled grunt, and quickly retreated back into the bush with the twins not far behind.

Surprisingly, we met up with the family of moose again while rounding the next bend. By this point the cow moose had had about enough of us and she lead the calves across to the opposite bank. Everything was fine until one of the calves began to cry out because it couldn't find a place to climb up on the shore. Mom decided then to hold her ground. With her ears turned back and hackles turned up, the cow moose charged toward our canoe. After that we tried every-thing to avoid her — passing on the far side, retreating back upriver, even speeding directly forward — and each time the cow moose would decide to charge toward us. Finally, Hugh and I stepped out of the canoe and dragged the boat through a nearby marsh, hoping it would eventually lead back to the river. It was a desperate measure — wading through boot-sucking muck with a high-ly aggressive moose on our tail — but the cow actually returned to her young and allowed us to safely rejoin the river.

Once we reached Sawbill Lake we took another break on an island camp-site to the north. When we checked out the site, my ever-increasing regret at not having staying over first at Ivanhoe Provincial Park or Red Pine Lodge before heading out on the river was confirmed. If you stay there first, your first night out can be had at Sawbill Lake — a far better place than the site where Hugh and I stayed on the small unnamed lake.

Not long after leaving Sawbill Lake by way of the northwest outlet, we ran our first major rapid. It was a rocky mess, especially with the water level close to summer drought conditions. (I've never seen such a dry spring.) But there was at least enough water to avoid having to use the 110-yard (100 m) portage on the left bank.

Again, low water levels turned the next rapid into a bump and grind. We decided it would be best if Hugh carried the two heavy packs up and over the 66-yard (60 m) portage to the right while I took the canoe down the far left chan-nel. In retrospect, I guess Hugh got a bum deal. But my 17-foot plastic We-no-nah isn't known for its turning ability, and at the time I figured it would be easier to make the tight turn at the bottom of the run by paddling the canoe solo.

A third rapid soon followed. The 220-yard (200 m) portage to the right could be cut in half by running the first shallow drop to a secondary (unmarked) take-out just above a totally unrunnable stretch. Hugh and I didn't even notice the secondary trail, however, until we had half our gear stored at the put-in. We decided saving such a short section of portage wasn't even worth the bother.

The out-of-date Ministry of Natural Resources guide we packed along marked the fourth rapid as "rapids with a strong current." But when Hugh and I approached the deceptively easy drop, then glanced at the incredibly steep take-out of the 372-yard (340 m) portage to the left, we tempted fate and headed straight down the rapid. What a mistake! After rounding the first bend we were forced out of the canoe and ended up taking almost a half-hour to line through a narrow, rocky gorge. The rapid is basically unrunnable in any water level. In fact, in spring floods it would be suicidal.

Two more rapids remain before the river reaches Halcrow Lake. The first is an easy swift with a hardly used 66-yard (60 m) portage to the left. The second is another story. It's been dubbed Run and Duck because of a number of cedar logs stretched out over the rapid. For some odd reason, this run has become the highlight of the trip for some extreme canoeists. Hugh and I, however, found it difficult enough to balance while lifting our canoe over the giant logjam just before the rapid, let alone attempt the limbo while flushing through funnel of whitewater. So we climbed down from the logjam and went back to use the easy 77-yard (70 m) portage marked to the right.

Halcrow Lake is excellent fishing. Hugh and I caught a mess of walleye and pike where the river twists to the southeast. We should have made camp on a choice site marked on the north shore, but a dead moose was floating nearby, bloated and covered in flies, and this natural form of bear bait forced us to continue on to the campsite at the falls below Vice Lake. It took more than two hours to reach the lake, running two shallow swifts and then carrying over two short portages (70 yards and 22 yards [65 m, 20 m]), both marked on the left. And we stopped to catch a few more walleye for diner directly below another small swift at the north end of the lake. So it was 7 p.m. by the time we carried over the 148-yard (135 m) portage marked to the left of the falls.

The campsite at the put-in was a shocking mess. It seemed some fishermen from one of the nearby fly-in camps had left a bag of garbage hung up on a tree and a neighboring bear had spread out the contents, made up of beer cans, paper plates and food scraps. Disgusted, we backtracked and set up camp on the opposite end of the portage. Our tent was set up beside a stored aluminum boat, but we were closer to the falls and enjoyed our fish-fry on a rock outcrop overlooking the 30-foot-high (9 m) cascade.

A little sore from the long paddle the day before, Hugh and I didn't get on our way until midmorning. Once past the falls we noticed the landscape begin to change, with more rock jutting out and the odd patch of red pine taking hold on soft, sandy beaches. We fished in one of the two bays to the north with little success (only three small pike) and then returned to the river where it traveled east, past a remote fishing camp, and then north toward Raney and Denyes Lake.

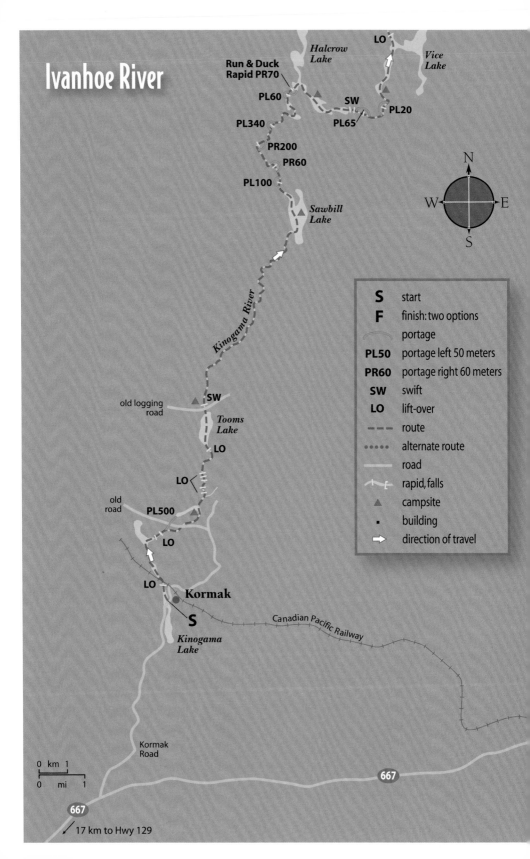

Ivanhoe River

Run & Duck Rapid PR70

Halcrow Lake

LO

Vice Lake

PL60

SW

PL65

PL20

PL340

PR200

PR60

PL100

Sawbill Lake

Kinogama River

old logging road

SW

Tooms Lake

LO

LO

old road

PL500

LO

LO

Kormak

S

Kinogama Lake

Canadian Pacific Railway

S	start
F	finish: two options
	portage
PL50	portage left 50 meters
PR60	portage right 60 meters
SW	swift
LO	lift-over
	route
	alternate route
	road
	rapid, falls
▲	campsite
▪	building
→	direction of travel

N

W — E

S

0 km 1

0 mi 1

Kormak Road

667

667

17 km to Hwy 129

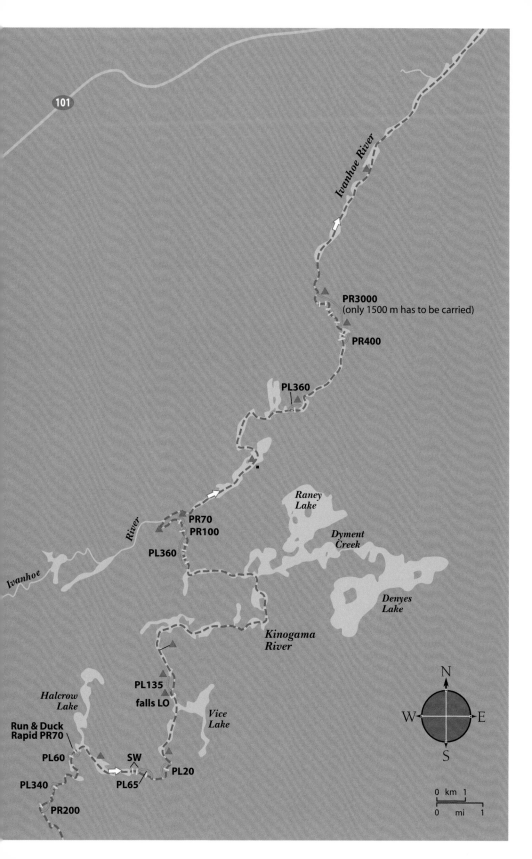

101

Ivanhoe River

PR3000
(only 1500 m has to be carried)

PR400

PL360

*Raney
Lake*

PR70
PR100

*Dyment
Creek*

PL360

River

Ivanhoe

*Denyes
Lake*

*Kinogama
River*

PL135

falls LO

*Vice
Lake*

*Halcrow
Lake*

Run & Duck
Rapid PR70

SW

PL60

PL20

PL340

PL65

PR200

N

W   E

S

0   km 1

0   mi   1

Ivanhoe River

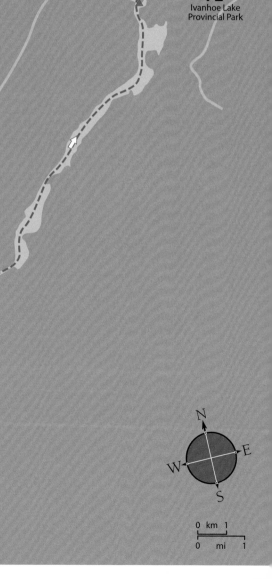

S   start
F   finish: two options
      portage
PL50   portage left 50 meters
PR60   portage right 60 meters
SW   swift
LO   lift-over
--- route
····· alternate route
    road
    rapid, falls
▲   campsite
▪   building
➡   direction of travel

Red Pine Lodge **F1**

Ivanhoe

Lake

F2
Ivanhoe Lake Provincial Park

Ivanhoe Provincial Park Road

101

101

101

Ivanhoe River

N
E
W
S

0   km   1
0   mi   1

We had planned to spend a day fishing both lakes and maybe find a bush site to spend the night on, but when we came to the entrance of Raney Lake, a total of five fishing boats loaded with anglers jigging for walleye were spread out across the opening. I figured the fishermen were more surprised to see us than we were to see them. Especially when one rowdy individual yelled out, "Where the hell did you come from?" After all, they probably spent a good buck to be flown in to what they perceived as the middle of nowhere. None of them knew about a town named Kormak or even a river named Kinogama. To be social, though, I did ask if they had had any luck. Immediately one of the bunch blurted out, "If I had to live off our catch, I'd be dead by now." To ease their frustrations, Hugh told them our luck had been just as bad, even though our total catch so far had added up to thirty-nine fish.

After sharing some excuses why the fish weren't biting, Hugh and I wished the group well and kept with the river rather than spend the day on Raney and Denyes Lake. It's not that we disliked running into the fly-in fishermen. They were actually a great bunch of guys. But knowing that they only had to step out of a Beaver or Cessna float plane to get there really irked us — and, personally, watching their powerboats buzz by us all day would have driven me mad.

The river turns east and forms almost a complete box before traveling north again. Then it's portage time again. The first is 394 yards (360 m), marked to the left, and heads straight up a mound of rock for 22 yards (20 m) before it begins to level out. Hugh and I carried the packs over first, but after catching a glimpse of the rapids on our return, we decided to run it. There were four drops altogether. The first drop was a little tricky and we decided at the last minute to jump out and line it. A log hanging low over the third drop also forced us to line again once again.

Close by were two more rapids. Both were runnable but had rough portages (110 yards and 77 yards [100 m, 70 m]) marked on the right bank.

The Kinogama meanders along for another 2 miles (3 km) before it meets up with the Ivanhoe. A campsite on the left bank, complete with an elaborate framework of pine to hang a tarp over, marks the junction of the two rivers. At first glance the Ivanhoe seems identical to the Kinogama. But the further you travel downstream, the more the Ivanhoe comes into its own, its weedy bays alive with pike and rocky cliffs crowned with pine and birch. It was still early when Hugh and I managed to paddle to the confluence of the Kinogama and Ivanhoe Rivers, so we continued on to where the Ivanhoe widens out, looking almost lake-like, and found a disappointing spot on a large island. It's not that it was a poor tent site. It's just that the camp was positioned directly across from another fishing lodge. Still, once the fishing boats had come in for the night, the spot seemed secluded enough, I guess.

We were on the water late the next morning, somewhat apprehensive about the 3,300-yard (3,000 m) portage waiting for us halfway through the day. Not far from our camp the river took a sharp turn to the east and then eventually twisted its way around to the west. Shortly after, where a large bay opens up to the north, a 394-yard (360 m) portage is found marked to the left of a double set of rapids. It comes complete with a scenic campsite located at the first of two possible put-ins. Hugh and I found it an easy carry. As usual, we took our packs across first, setting them down at the first put-in, and then checked out the run on the return visit. Because of low water, it was another technical rock-garden, with a choice between two S-bend channels. We took the one to the right, bumped only once halfway down, and eddied in at the campsite to grab our packs.

From here the river spreads out and meanders for at least another hour before a 440-yard (400 m) portage is marked to the right. A quick look from the take-out ruled out the rapid as unrunnable, but there were a number of trees fallen across the first quarter of the portage, so Hugh and I walked down the right shore and checked it out anyway. Halfway down we were convinced that the rapid was a mess. A jumble of giant rocks and splashing foam stood before us. There wasn't even a safe place to line down, so we took our lumps on the unmaintained portage.

After the 440-yard (400 m) portage, the river pools and then twists its way to the left, toward the infamous 2-mile (3 km) carry. A poor campsite marks the take-out on the right bank, and almost immediately the trail heads up a hill for a good 330 yards (300 m). The portage also leads away from the river here, making it impossible to even scout the rapid until you're about a quarter of the way along. When it does rejoin the river, the portage stays dangerously close to the edge of a high esker, overlooking an extremely technical stretch of white-water. After about another 550 yards (500 m) or so the main portage leads away from the river again and a side trail climbs down to the end of the last difficult set of rapids. Canoeists can continue on the main portage, contending with only one last hill before the put-in, or make use of a side trail and run and wade the second half, which is made up of cobblestone and straightforward route choices. Hugh and I took the second choice and saved almost 1,650 yards (1,500 m) of portaging.

What remains is Ivanhoe Lake. For the most part it's narrow. But it's also 22 miles (36 km) in length and aligned perfectly with the prevailing winds. As well, only two designated campsites are on the lake: one about 3 miles (5 km) from the end of the 3,300-yard (3,000 m) portage and the other about 3 miles (5 km) from the docks of Red Pine Lodge

It was 1 p.m. when Hugh and I reached the first campsite. Feeling a little fatigued from the last portage, we seriously considered calling it a day. At the time, however, the wind happened to be coming from the south — something no canoeist should ever pass up when paddling such a large lake. So we went for it, and eight hours later dragged ourselves to shore to make our final camp only an hour's paddle away from the take-out.

TIME 4 to 5 days

DIFFICULTY Because this route is no longer being maintained it can be grueling at times. However, when considering only rapids and portage lengths, it's classified a novice trip.

PORTAGES 15

LONGEST PORTAGE
3,300 yards (3,000 m); only half of that must be carried over

BEST TIME TO RUN IT
Spring through fall

FEE The route travels through Crown land, where no fee is required for Canadian citizens. However, a moderate fee is charged for the shuttle.

ALTERNATIVE ROUTE None

OUTFITTERS
Red Pine Lodge
Box 94
Foleyet, Ontario
P0M 1T0
705-899-2875

Missinaibi Outfitters
Box 1207
Collingwood, Ontario
L9Y 3Y9
705-444-7836
(off season)
or
Racine Lake
Chapleau, Ontario
P0M 1K0
705-864-2065
(May to September)
www.missinaibi.com

FOR MORE INFORMATION
Ivanhoe Lake Provincial Park
Ministry of Natural Resources
190 Cherry Street
Chapleau, Ontario
P0M 1K0
705-899-2633 (park office)
1-888-668-7275 (reservations)

MAPS Red Pine Lodge and the Ministry of Natural Resources have produced a pamphlet entitled *Pishkanogami Canoe Route — Kormak to Foleyet via the Kinogama and Ivanhoe Rivers.*

TOPOGRAPHIC MAPS
41 O/11, 41 O/15, 42 B/2 & 42B/1
Provincial Series: Scale 1:100,000
Ridout 410/NE & Foleyet 42B/SE

*Mark finds the mother of all kettle holes along the
Lady Evelyn Falls portage.*

Lake Superior's Sand River

THE SAND RIVER is similar to most rivers that flow into the expanse of Lake Superior; it twists its way around gravel bars and tumbles over sheer granite. The difference, however, is that this route allows canoeists with only moderate whitewater experience to enjoy the splendor of the rocky headlands east of Ontario's freshwater sea.

Some canoeists access the Sand by heading out from Mijinemungshing Lake and, by using Lake Superior Provincial Park's Old Woman Lake Route, they follow a chain of lakes for two days before connecting up with the river. Others choose to head up to the headwaters by taking the Algoma Central Railway. I've tried both routes and much prefer starting off the trip with a scenic train ride through the Agawa Canyon instead of finding myself windbound on Mijinemungshing Lake or slogging through the mucky portages found just before the river.

The train can be boarded at Sault Ste. Marie, Hawk Junction (14 miles [22 km] east of Wawa) or Frater Station, near Agawa Bay. Frater Station is your best choice, especially as it is the closest to the trip's take-out. Recently, however, the station has been left abandoned and the 5-mile (8 km) Frater Road is no longer maintained, making the drive in from the highway a bit of a challenge. Check with the train service or local outfitters to see if this is still an option.

Before you head out on the train, a second vehicle must be dropped off at the take-out. Drive north on Highway 17 to the Sand River Road, located just south of the bridge. Then turn right and follow the 1.25-mile (2 km) dirt road to a designated parking lot. Shuttle services are also available through Dan Miles (705-882-2183) or Dan Grenier (705-882-2159). Both will either drive you directly to Frater Station, which saves your vehicle some wear and tear on the Frater Station Road, or pick your vehicle up at the train station parking lot and have it waiting for you at the take-out by the end of your trip.

Train tickets for passengers and freight can be purchased in Sault Ste. Marie or from the train's conductor (it's a few dollars cheaper at the train station). To get information about fares and train schedules call 705-946-7300 or 1-800-242-9287. And since you're traveling through Lake Superior Provincial Park, an interior camping permit must be picked up at the Agawa Bay Campground.

Even more difficult than accessing the river is choosing when to paddle it. Spring floods can leave portage landings dangerously close to whatever you're trying to avoid. In low water conditions, you might find yourself walking a dry stream bed most of the way. I find the first week in June is a happy medium. Just pray the blackflies haven't hatched yet!

The train ride through the canyon lasts about an hour and a half, taking you through the same breathtaking scenery that members of the Group of Seven once captured on canvas while traveling the same rail service. Then, without much warning, the conductor will announce your stop — Mile 136 $^1/_4$, a bay on the southeast side of Sand Lake — and before you know it you're left stranded, with no way back except the river.

From the tracks a short trail heads down to the lake. Then, from the put-in, the route heads east, directly across the lake, and south to the far end where you choose one of two portages leading to the river. To the extreme right is a 16-yard (15 m) carry-over to a small beaver pond that drains directly into the Sand; to the left is a 180-yard (165 m) path, marked to the right of a makeshift dam constructed in 1956 by Junior Rangers. The first portage sounds easier but the second is more straightforward, and the first half of it is runnable.

Two more portages (660 yards and 170 yards [600 m, 155 m]) are soon to follow. The first is a bit of a climb and marked to the far right of a log-choked chute, and the second is a tough carry over some uprooted spruce trees. Both sections of rapids make excellent feeding grounds for trout and offer a perfect place for anglers to wet a line. An even better fishing spot, however, is 1.25 miles (2 km) downstream at the base of a small cascade. Here, a 800-yard (750 m) portage is marked to the left and comes with a campsite directly at the take-out.

I spent my first night here while traveling the Sand River in 1997, partnered up with Mark Robbins, a fellow instructor from Sir Sandford Fleming College. We cast for trout rising for flies at a section of quiet water directly in front of our campsite, and later on dined on pan-fried trout caught just a stone's throw away from our evening fire.

A fifth portage begins directly across from where the fourth portage ends. The 465-yard (425 m) trail avoids a total of five swifts. It's an easy carry, but if there's enough water to keep your canoe from dragging across the cobble bottom then I suggest you run it. Not too far downstream is a trickier set of rapids, however. It can be run by experienced canoeists, but even in the best of conditions some of the rocks are unavoidable. Be safe and carry your gear over the 600-yard (550 m) portage marked on the left first and then use the logging bridge halfway along to scout the rapids.

The Sand meanders almost unbearably from here, and may be a monotonous stretch of river for some. It's in calm sections such as this, however, that wildlife abounds. Dozens of tiny warblers (common yellow-throats, red starts, yellow warblers) can be spotted darting in and out of patches of alder and dogwood, and the small back bays are good places to watch for moose.

Eventually two sets of rapids help break up the boredom, the first a double drop with a 223-yard (205 m) portage marked on the left, and the second a set of gravel rapids with a 110-yard (100 m) portage also marked on the left. Then, not far beyond where the river widens its banks, you'll encounter a total of six portages before coming to where the Old Woman Lake Route joins in. The first two (165 yards and 99 yards [150 m, 90 m]) are marked on the right, and the remaining portages (372 yards, 350 yards, 50 yards and 120 yards [340 m, 320 m, 45 m, 110 m]) are all found on the left. Take note, however, that during good water levels, the second, third and fourth are possible to run.

From here only four more portages remain before you can call it a day at Calwin Falls — a 220-yard (200 m) and 104-yard (95 m) on the left, followed quickly by a 66-yard (60 m) on the right, and a final 80-yard (75 m) back on the left. At the falls there's an exceptional campsite close to the drop, marked about a quarter of the way along the 242-yard (220 m) portage on the left.

From Calwin Falls to the even more impressive Lady Evelyn Falls, it's only half a day's paddle. The section of river in between has only five portages — a 330-yard (300 m) and 104-yard (95 m) marked to the left, not far downstream from Calwin Falls, and a 33-yard, 27-yard and 110-yard (30 m, 25 m, 100 m) marked on the right, just before Lady Evelyn Falls.

On my trip down the Sand with canoe mate Mark Robbins, this section of river was my all-round favorite stretch. We simply drifted with the soft current, passing high gravel banks on one side and deep pools, chock-full of brook trout, on the other. To me, it was a paradise that only an angler as obsessed as I am with catching elusive brookies could ever possibly understand.

A 1,200-yard (1,100 m) portage, marked on the left of Lady Evelyn Falls, is not only the longest portage en route, it also is the most treacherous, especially when rains grease up the rocks. But it is a fantastic place to camp. There's not a bad site near the take-out (look for the exceptional collection of kettle holes formed in the rock nearby), but a second one, approximately halfway along the trail, is much nicer. Don't put in here, though. There's still a good rush of water around the next bend.

The swift water continues past Lady Evelyn Falls (two 99-yard [90 m] portages may be used on the right). As the river makes a sharp turn to the north, a challenging set of Class II rapids can be run along the right-hand side by experienced canoeists. However, an easy 292-yard (265 m) portage does exist on the right. At the base of the run, where you can either squeeze between a tight chute or take your chances on the rock garden to the far left, is a sheer granite cliff rising out from the water, majestic above the river.

From here it's a joyride if water levels are high, allowing you to pass through an almost continuous set of gravel swifts. But if the water levels drop in the slightest, you're forced to use a poorly maintained 550-yard (500 m) portage found along the left bank, about half a mile (1 km) from the last cliff site, and then wade or line down the shallow rapids that continue almost right up to two stunted falls, both of which must be portaged, 292 yards and 365 yards (265 m, 335 m) on the right.

It's just a ten-minute paddle before you reach the take-out point. A 148-yard (135 m) trail will lead you uphill to the parking lot, not far from where the Sand River takes a final plunge before it empties out into the expanse of Lake Superior.

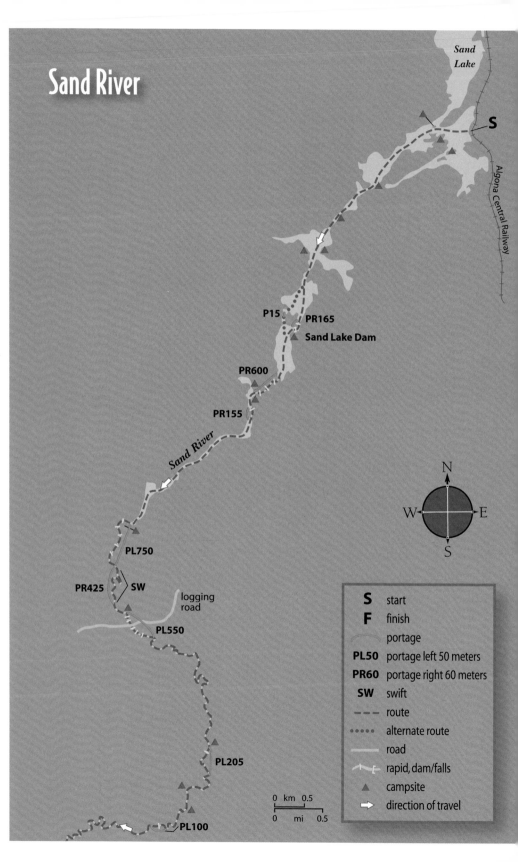

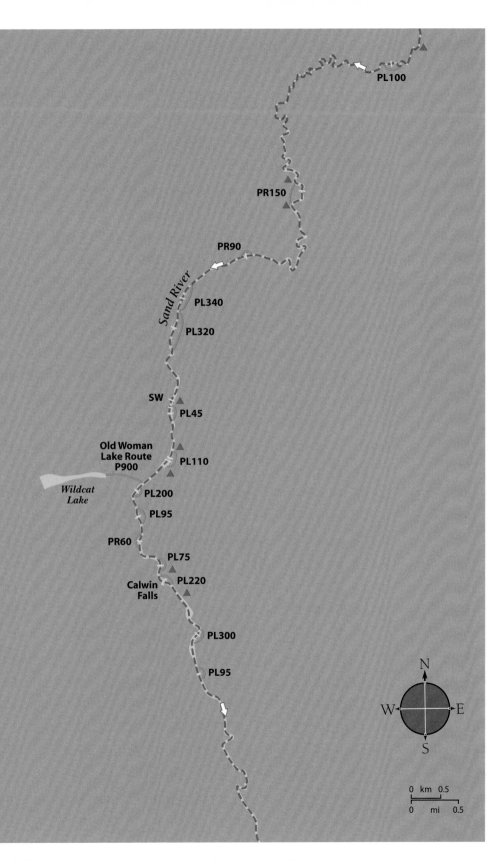

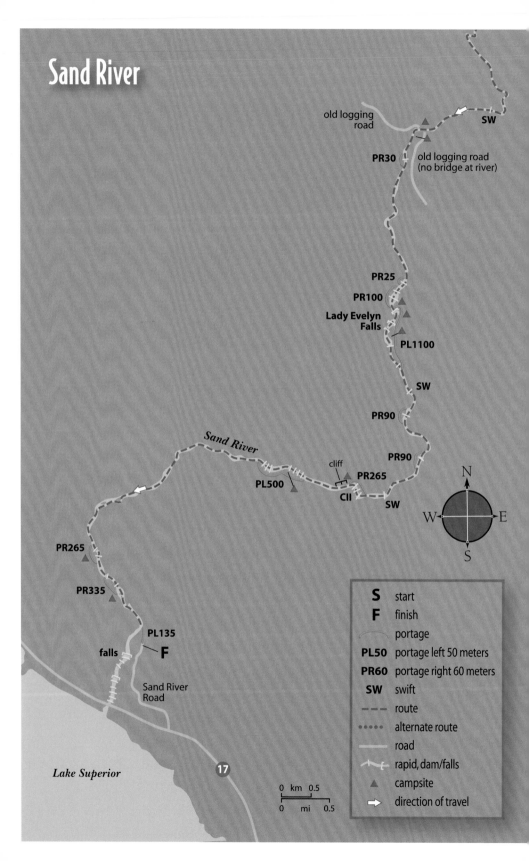

Sand River

old logging road

SW

PR30
old logging road
(no bridge at river)

PR25

PR100

Lady Evelyn
Falls

PL1100

SW

PR90

Sand River

PR90

cliff

PR265

PL500

CII

SW

N

W — E

S

PR265

PR335

PL135

falls

F

Sand River
Road

Lake Superior

17

0   km   0.5

0   mi   0.5

S	start
F	finish
	portage
PL50	portage left 50 meters
PR60	portage right 60 meters
SW	swift
- - -	route
·····	alternate route
	road
⌁⌁	rapid, dam/falls
▲	campsite
➞	direction of travel

Lake Superior's Sand River

TIME 4 to 5 days

DIFFICULTY Most rapids can be portaged and therefore only moderate tripping skills are required.

PORTAGES 29

LONGEST PORTAGE
1,200 yards (1,100 m)

BEST TIME TO RUN IT
Spring only

FEE An interior camping permit must be purchased at Agawa Bay Campground for travel in Lake Superior Provincial Park. There's also a fee for train tickets if you choose to access the river by rail and a charge for shuttling your vehicle to the take-out.

ALTERNATIVE ROUTE Some canoeists head out from Mijinemungshing Lake, accessed from Highway 17 via Mijinemungshing Road, and use the Old Woman Lake Route to join the river just before Calwin Falls.

OUTFITTERS
Dan Grenier
705-882-2159
or
Dan Miles
705-882-2183
Highway 17 North
Montreal River Harbour, Ontario
P0S 1H0

Naturally Superior
R.R. 1 Lake Superior
Wawa, Ontario
P0S 1K0
1-800-203-9092 or 705-856-2989
rock@naturallysuperior.com
www.naturallysuperior.com

FOR MORE INFORMATION
Lake Superior Provincial Park
Box 267
Wawa, Ontario
P0S 1K0
705-856-2284

Algoma Central Railway Inc.
Passenger Sales
Box 130, 129 Bay Street
Sault Ste. Marie, Ontario
P6A 6Y2
705-946-7300
1-800-242-9287
www.agawacanyontourtrain.com

MAPS The Ministry of Natural Resources has produced a canoe route pamphlet titled *Canoeing in Lake Superior Provincial Park*, which describes a number of possible routes in the park, including the Old Woman Lake Route.

TOPOGRAPHIC MAPS
41 N/7, 41 N/10 & 41 N/11

The Turtle River
Home of the White Otter Castle

IN JULY OF 1998, ALANA AND I SPENT A WEEK PADDLING THE TURTLE RIVER, a 100-mile-long (160 km) provincial waterway park located north of Quetico Park and south of the town of Ignace. Apart from spotting twelve bald eagles and two golden eagles, spending an entire afternoon paddling through a bed of wild rice, and leaving an offering of tobacco at half-a-dozen Native pictographs, the highlight of our travels down this remote river was making a special pilgrimage to Jimmy McOuat's White Otter Castle — a place that is one of the most mysterious hermitages of the north.

Alana and I were certainly not the first to visit White Otter Castle; this 28-by-38-foot log castle built entirely by a sixty-year-old hermit eight decades earlier has been a local drawing card for years. One of the first visitors was canoeist C. L. Hodson, working on an article for *Rod and Gun* magazine in 1914.

"Mile after mile of rugged shoreline drops behind and then about 2:30 p.m. 'Old Jimmy's Place' quite suddenly slips into view. A hundred yards back from the lake it stands, on the edge of a small clearing. In the background are dark pine woods. No one speaks but with one accord the paddles pause here. Eyes strain. Heartbeats quicken. In the very air is mystery. Almost, we fear to approach this retreat of the wild man. We are intruders — trespassers. Then, slowly, the paddles dip. The bow grates on a strip of sandy beach. Gingerly we step ashore and approach the hermitage."

I felt a little gypped after reading about Hodson's visit. Sure, the castle itself is impressive — standing four stories high and made of 200 pine logs, averaging 37 feet (16.5 yards) long. But what made Hodson's arrival better than ours was that "Old Jimmy" was home at the time. And, intrigued by all the stories told about why the hermit (his name was pronounced McQuat) built the bizarre monument (one of the most poetic, about a mail-order bride who canceled the deal because Jimmy lacked a proper house), Hodson was able to ask the builder himself.

It seems it all had to do with being falsely accused of throwing a corn cob at a bad-tempered schoolmaster (it was actually Jimmy's chum who threw the corn). For some reason, he was never able to forget the curse given out by the angry man: "Jimmy McOuat — Ye'll never do any good! Ye'll die in a shack!" And, decades later, Jimmy found his accursed prophecy unfolding. After gambling his life savings away on a failed gold rush, he found himself on the shores of the remote White Otter Lake (known then as Big Clearwater Lake), living in a shack. "All the time I lived in a shack," Jimmy told Hodson, "I kept thinking — I must build me a house. And so I have. Ye couldn't call this a shack, could ye?"

In 1918, four years after Hodson's visit, Jimmy McOuat drowned while netting fish in front of his castle. His partially decomposed body, wrapped up in fish netting, was found the next spring by forest rangers and buried beside his beloved wilderness home. So Alana and I thought the only way, other than conjure up Jimmy's ghost, to capture the true spirit of White Otter Castle would be to have Dennis Smyk — president of the Friends of White Otter Castle and owner of Dream Catcher Tours — give us a personal tour.

Traditionally canoeists visit White Otter Castle by paddling for two days south of Ignace (check map for access points and route description), making use of the same fifteen portages that Jimmy carried twenty-six windows over to complete his castle. Alana and I, however, wimped out and had Dennis boat us across Clearwater West Lake and then White Otter Lake (access by turning east off Highway 622 onto Clear Lake West Road, and then left to Browns Clearwater West Lodge).

After a day of exploring a few of White Otter Lake's twenty-three rock painting sites, a logging camp that once served as a prisoner-of-war camp, the site of an old ranger station, and a guided walk through the castle, Alana and I unpacked our canoe gear from the boat and bid farewell to our private interpreter, paddling ourselves across to a nearby island to make camp for the first night.

Jimmy McOuat was buried in front of his four-story-high White Otter Castle.

It was bear-phobia that kept us from making use of a campsite just down the beach from the castle; we figured problem bruins would love to hang out at such a busy tourist spot. As soon as we pulled up on shore, however, Alana and I discovered that dozens of other campers had thought the same. Garbage and fresh mounds of toilet paper littered the site. The food scraps, fishing line, candy wrappers and eggshells were immediately dealt with by burning them in the firepit. But the piles of human waste still made camping on the island unpleasant, to say the least, especially when we discovered that our dog, Bailey, had an unfortunate habit of fetching poo. To make matters worse, when I went to scold her, my left foot found a fresh pile. I must have washed my sandal a dozen times.

Needless to say, Alana and I left the island campsite early the next day, and arrived at our first portage well before 8 a.m. There's a choice of two trails to take you around to the right of an old logging sluice. From the rough campsite marked at the take-out, a 252-yard (230 m) portage heads down a steep slope to the left and a 580-yard (530 m) portage heads up a hill to the right. At first glance, the shorter trail seems easier. Don't bother, however. The longer 580-yard (530 m) portage is much more direct and far less strenuous.

The portage leads you into Unnamed Lake, a scenic spot with round boulders sticking out everywhere. It looks as if a child's bag of marbles had been spilled out along the shoreline. Look for one rock in particular that holds a rusted logging pin that once supported a boom across the expanse of the lake. For three years (1912–15) a logging company attempted to flush sawlogs down the Turtle, at the same time almost flooding poor Jimmy's castle. "About seven feet of bank at my door is washed away," he wrote the Lands office in 1915, "All on account of a thickheaded lumberjack. Does the law allow one man to drown another or to destroy his property and him just stand with his hands in his pockets when there is a few sticks [dynamite] within reach that would put the dam out of business?" Ironically, however, it was the high cost and especially the time it took (a total of three years) to send the logs down such a meandering river, and not Jimmy's threat of civil disobedience, that put a stop to the flooding.

An easy 580-yard (530 m) portage — complete with an old trapper's shack halfway along — is marked well to the right of the next set of sluiceways. It takes you into the east bay of Dibble Lake. All across the lake are sandy beaches and rocky islands, each one of them an ideal lunch spot. Alana and I were fighting a strong northwest wind, however, and we chose to skip lunch and make the long haul along Dibble's north shore before the wind become unbearable.

By midday we had carried our gear over the 55-yard (50 m) portage found to the right of yet another sluiceway, and then stopped for our first break of the day at a pictograph site (an adult moose and a tally mark) located on the rock face to the left of the second bay, just before the entrance to Smirch Lake.

Smirch Lake is more bowl-shaped than Dibble, and with the northwest wind still building, it was becoming increasingly difficult for Alana and I to cross. The only thing that kept us going was that three-quarters the way along, on the west shore, was a 660-yard (600 m) portage that serves as a shortcut to where the waterway bends around and begins heading directly south. Once over the portage, Alana and I knew we could finally take advantage of the prevailing winds and make up the time we lost on the two large lakes.

Not far downstream from the put-in of the 660-yard (600 m) portage is the first rapid that's not blocked by a logging sluiceway. A 350-yard (320 m) portage is marked on the left bank, but Alana and I made a precision run just to the right of a large boulder set in midstream, and then eddied to the left to make use of the designated campsite marked on an outcrop of rock.

Two pictographs decorate the wall of rock lining the right bank; the first is above the rapid and is so faded that it's hard to distinguish. The second, situated a few yards below the rapid and almost directly across from the campsite, is a clear illustration of a turtle with what appears to be a canoe emerging from its body, and is most likely the reason for the river's name.

The next morning's paddle was almost dreamlike, with the mist hanging low over the river as we skirted the top end of Pekagoning Lake and right up until we carried over the 130-yard (120 m) island portage at Twin Falls.

Not far from the falls is the Highway 622 bridge (an alternative access point), and beyond the paved road the change in environment couldn't become more dramatic. Hard granite is replaced almost completely by sand until just after the Wapageisi River flows in from the north and a long stretch of rapids mark the approach to Turtle Falls.

At first the river is simply squeezed between two rock points and the swift water that's formed can hardly be counted as a rapid. Almost immediately after, however, a 252-yard (230 m) portage is marked to the right of some rougher water that can quickly become a mess during a dry spell.

Next up was a shallow section that twisted from right to left and then center, followed by a quick swift and then four major drops. A tight corner, with a souse hole bellowing up at the bottom, kept us from running the first of the four drops. We lifted over on the left before completing the run. (A bush trail on the left bank continues on if you wish to avoid all four drops.)

Then finally comes Turtle Falls, with a campsite up on a knoll to the left marking the take-out for the 306-yard (280 m) portage. It's not a bad trail until the steep slope at the end, and it comes complete with a side trail leading to a scenic lookout three-quarters of the way along.

The river doesn't speed up again until an hour past Turtle Falls, where it tumbles over a small cascade. A quick 44-yard (40 m) portage is marked to the right. Then, another half-hour downstream, Alana and I came to a short rapid that wasn't marked on our government map. It was an easy run, but for the remainder of the trip I felt I couldn't totally trust the park's guide.

We came to another stretch of fast water just after the river turned to the southwest. Two sets run close together. The first rapid is a double run (Alana and I found the second drop questionable and used a poorly marked 88-yard

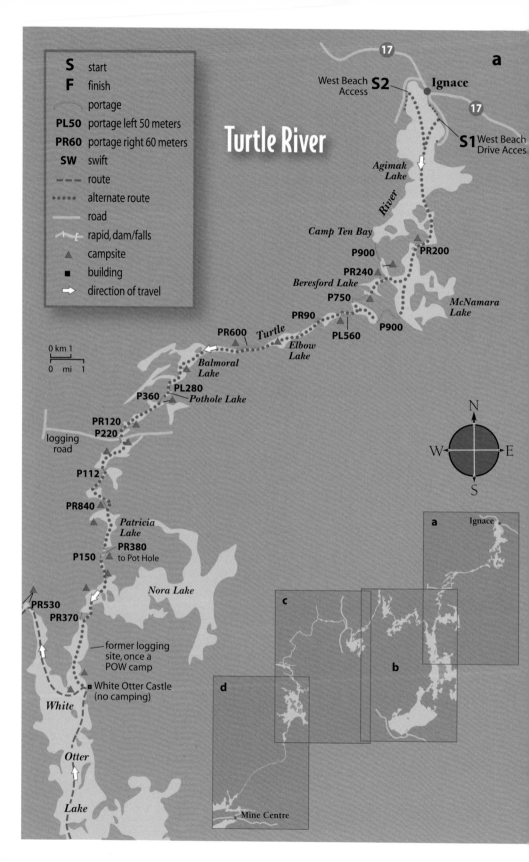

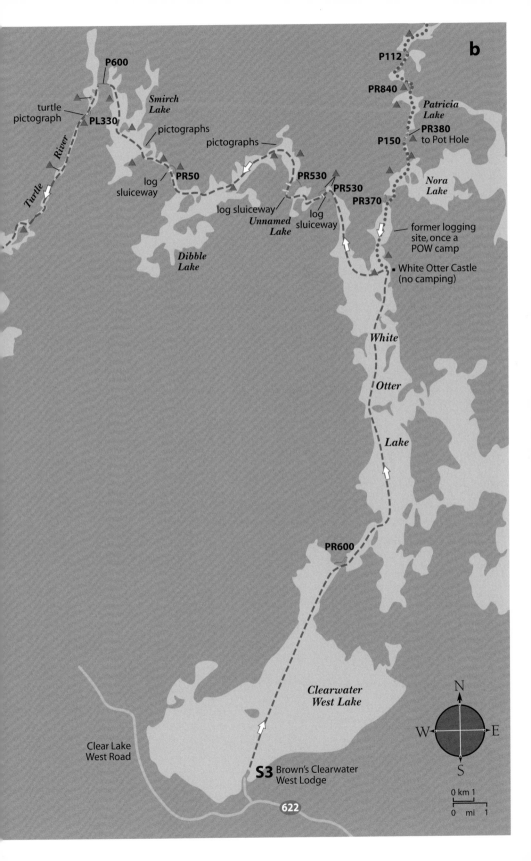

b

turtle
pictograph

Turtle River

P600

PL330

Smirch Lake

pictographs

pictographs

log
sluiceway

PR50

log sluiceway

Unnamed Lake

log
sluiceway

PR530

PR530

PR370

Dibble Lake

P112

PR840

Patricia Lake

PR380
to Pot Hole

P150

Nora Lake

former logging
site, once a
POW camp

• White Otter Castle
(no camping)

White

Otter

Lake

PR600

Clearwater West Lake

Clear Lake
West Road

S3 Brown's Clearwater
West Lodge

622

N
W — E
S

0 km 1
0   mi   1

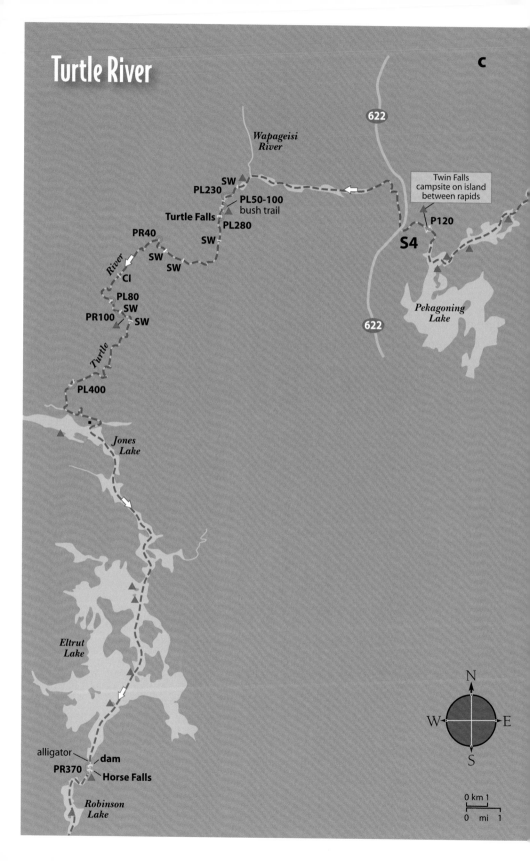

Turtle River

C

622

Wapageisi River

SW
PL230
PL50-100
bush trail
Turtle Falls
PL280
SW
PR40
SW
River
SW
CI
PL80
SW
PR100
SW
Turtle
PL400

Twin Falls
campsite on island
between rapids

P120
S4

Pekagoning Lake

622

Jones Lake

Eltrut Lake

alligator
dam
PR370
Horse Falls

Robinson Lake

N
W E
S

0 km 1
0 mi 1

Turtle River

S start
F finish
portage
PL50 portage left 50 meters
PR60 portage right 60 meters
SW swift
--- route
..... alternate route
road
rapid, dam/falls
▲ campsite
▪ building
➡ direction of travel

Eltrut Lake

alligator   **dam**
PR370   **Horse Falls**

Robinson Lake

PL400

PR60

▪ old shack

SW

PL100 CII

PL100
bush trail

Heron River

Little Turtle Lake

Mine Centre

F Public Launch

N
W — E
S

11

Bad Vermillion Lake

11

0 km 1
0 mi 1

d

[80 m] portage on the left). The next is a long set with an obvious route choice close to the left bank. A 110-yard (100 m) portage is marked on the right, but Alana and I found enough courage to run the entire rapid this time. We finally called it a day at a nice campsite located at the end of the portage.

The morning of the fourth day was brisk, so we took time out to light our first breakfast fire of the trip, using one side to warm up our soggy boots and the other to fry up a four-pound walleye Alana caught at the base of the rapids.

A couple of hours were spent paddling downriver to Jones Lake, where we encountered a small swift just beyond our campsite and, further along, a good-size ledge followed by some extremely technical rapids. After scouting from shore, we guessed the bottom rapids could only be run if the water was high, so we stayed to the left after the initial take-out and made full use of the 440-yard (400 m) portage marked to the left.

Soon after, where alder flats take over thick stands of black spruce and a few patches of tamarack, a small creek empties into the Turtle River from the west and the waterway makes a dramatic turn to the left. Then, after a good twenty minutes of monotonous paddling, the river twists again, this time to the south-west toward Jones Lake, and then immediately to the southeast. The route out of Jones Lake, however, is almost totally obscured by swamp grass and wild rice. Alana and I, having missed the exit, paddled three-quarters the way across the lake before realizing our mistake. Even when we did retrace our steps and eventually continue on down the river, however, the route looked nothing like the topo map, and it wasn't until we entered the top end of Eltrut Lake (Turtle spelled backward) that I was certain of our whereabouts.

The labyrinth, however, happened to be a haven for wildlife, and we managed to spot two golden eagles and half-a-dozen turkey vultures; the V-shape pattern of the vulture's wingspan was the only way Alana and I could distinguish between the two species while they soared high above us.

Eltrut Lake is full of sunken islands, dead-end inlets and huge beds of emergent water plants, so navigation remained a challenge as we made our way across. Luckily, there wasn't a strong wind to content with, which could have been a major hazard on the lower half of the lake. By mid-afternoon we were paddling down the southern outlet, taking time to check out an abandoned alligator beached on the west shore, just before to the take-out for the 350-yard (320 m) portage to the right of Horse Falls.

The alligator, also known as a logger's warp tug, was one of the first labor-saving devices brought into the bush camps during the late nineteenth century. The steam-powered scow took over the job of oarsmen, who, with a pointer boat, would haul giant log-booms across a remote lake such as Eltrut. A powerful winch, equipped with a mile of steel cable and a strong anchor, was also placed on the bow, allowing the boat to haul itself overland.

Horse Falls was a scenic spot, and a prime campsite was located near the base. But because the water was so low, a strong stench of rotten fish polluted the air below the cascade, and Alana and I decided to paddle further downstream to make use of an island campsite on Robinson Lake. The moment we landed, however, all three of us were attacked by a swarm of angry wasps. Alana was stung twice on the hand, Bailey once on the eyelid and twice behind the ear, and I on my big toe.

We shoved off immediately and, after administering first aid to poor Bailey's eye, searched for an alternative site. The lake offered no other place to erect a tent, however, and we were actually forced back to the island to use a makeshift site on the far opposite end. I guess the upper section of the river had bewitched us with its rocky islands, elongated beaches, and campsites that couldn't be bettered until the next one came along. Now we found ourselves learning to enjoy a different environment, one of endless marsh, silt-colored water, and the lack of any decent places to call it a night.

To leave Robinson Lake the next morning, Alana and I used a 440-yard (400 m) portage that, at the take-out, climbed high up on the left bank, and then continued along a bush road until it turned back down to the river. Then,

Once past Horse Falls, Alana and I found ourselves paddling through a totally different environment — one that, unfortunately, lacked decent campsites.

once up and over a short 66-yard (60 m) portage on the right, we were back on the river, where once again the vegetation growing along the banks takes on a dramatic change. Instead of the common boreal species — typified by jack pine, black spruce and balsam fir — rare occurrences of southern species such as oak, green ash and silver maple begin to appear.

As in the upper reaches of the river, loggers also attempted to gather logs from the lower portion during the 1940s (look for the remains of an old wooden bridge and an abandoned cabin hunkered back in the woods beside a side stream). Luckily, however, most of the trees along the bank were left untouched, and the ones that were cut have now been replaced by second growth, leaving this unique habitat to continue to dominate the landscape all the way down to the take-out.

You have to run three more sets of rapids, beginning about a three-hour paddle from Robinson Lake, before you enter Little Turtle Lake. The first is made up of four drops that quickly follow one after the other, increasing in volume as they go. The second is an extremely technical Class II that comes with a 110-yard (100 m) portage on the left. And finally, there's a snakelike, rock-strewn rapid that rates as a moderate Class I with an optional 110-yard (100 m) bush trail on the left.

Muddy banks continued to dominate the riverbank. Alana and I couldn't find a single spot where we could place a tent. So we paddled to Little Turtle Lake, only to find fishing lodges or family cottages taking over every possible site. By the time we had reached the far eastern inlet, leading toward the town of Mine Center (turn right directly off Highway 11, and then stay right, keeping to the main road), we had to finally admit to ourselves that our life on the river was now over. Alana and I sadly made our way down the inlet, looking for the public boat launch where Dennis had promised he would park our vehicle.

The Turtle River: Home of the White Otter Castle

TIME 5 to 7 days

PORTAGES 27

LONGEST PORTAGE
920 yards (840 m)

DIFFICULTY Only novice whitewater experience is needed, but because the route is remote you should have at least moderate tripping skills.

BEST TIME TO RUN IT
Spring through fall

FEE The Turtle River is an unmaintained provincial park, and no camping permit is required for canoeing the river. A moderate fee is charge to shuttle your vehicle or access White Otter Lake by boat.

ALTERNATIVE ROUTE The traditional route begins at Ignace but a good number of portages can be cut off by having an outfitter boat you up to White Otter Lake from Clearwater West Lake or you can choose to begin at the Highway 622 bridge and reduce the trip to four days.

OUTFITTERS

Dream Catcher Tours
Dennis Smyk
153 Balsam Street
Box 989
Ignace, Ontario
P0T 1T0
807-934-6482

Browns' Clearwater West Lodge
Box 1766
Dep't. I
Atikokan, Ontario
P0T 1C0
807-597-2884
www.brownsclearwaterlodge.com

Soft Wilderness Adventures
Box 2080
Atikokan, Ontario
P0T 1C0
807-597-1377

Canoe Canada Outfitters
Box 1810
Atikokan, Ontario
P0T 1C0
807-597-6418
www.gordonsguide.com

Agimak Lake Resort
Box 188
Ignace, Ontario
P0T 1T0
May to October 807-934-2891
November to April 204-257-6353
www.agimaklake.com

FOR MORE INFORMATION
The Friends Of White Otter Castle
Box 2096
Atikokan, Ontario
P0T 1C0
807-934-6482

Ministry of Natural Resources
Box 448
Ignace, Ontario
P0T 1T0
807-934-2233

MAPS The Ministry of Natural Resources has produced an excellent canoe route map for the Turtle River.

TOPOGRAPHIC MAPS
52 F/8, 52 G/5, 52 G/4 & 52 F/1
Provincial Series: Scale 1:100,000
Gulliver River 52 G/SW, Gold Rock
52 F/SE & Seine River 52 C/NE

Twin Falls, Dumoine River.

The Dumoine River

BECAUSE I WAS THE CHIEF PHOTOGRAPHER OF THE GROUP, my canoe partner, Scott Roberts, and I had the privilege to take the first flight into the Dumoine River's Lac Laforge. While we stood beside our pile of camping gear, waiting for our pilot, Ron Bowes of Bradley Air Service, to taxi the plane toward the dock, it felt as if we were standing in line for a roller-coaster ride at an amusement park. Scott and I chatted about how easy the river should be for us, since we had already conquered other more seemingly wild rivers. Then the moment the pilot took off and we caught the first glimpse of the river tumbling down toward the Ottawa, I immediately popped an anti-nausea pill and began questioning the reason for climbing on board in the first place!

In twenty-five minutes the plane landed on the lower portion of Lac Laforge. While Scott and I waited for the others to arrive we practiced our paddle strokes out on the open water, hoping to regain some of our confidence. We thought it was good idea as well to rehearse our moves without the others looking on. You see, Len, Roy and Rick had already traveled down the Dumoine half-a-dozen times — all during spring flood — and had become masters at maneuvering through foaming whitewater. Compared to them, Scott and I were babes in the woods.

Even though a few canoeists try to drive to the Dumoine by using a network of logging roads, it's far better to fly in, and Bradley Air Service (613-586-2374) is your best choice. To reach them, turn off Highway 17 onto Swisha Road (the local name for Rapides-des-Joachims), just before the town of Rolphton. Then keep right, pass over the Ottawa River bridge, and drive down the hill behind the Esso gas station. Shuttles to either Driftwood Provincial Park or Pine Valley Camp, both located directly across from where the Dumoine River empties out into the Ottawa, can be arranged through Bradley Air Services as well. Our group decided on Driftwood Provincial Park because they didn't charge us a docking fee, but I'm not sure how long that will last.

It took our pilot a total of three flights to have all five of us gathered on the lake, and by the time we checked out the two logging "alligators" left to rust on the west shore and then headed down to the south end of Lac Laforge, it was late afternoon. So, after quickly portaging around two sets of falls (the first cascade has a 220-yard (200 m) portage to the right and the second, a 165-yard [150 m] portage to the left) and then paddling downriver for half an hour, we made camp.

Relatively speaking, it was still too early to end the day. But Roy and Rick had planned a birthday celebration for Len. Joke gifts were handed out (a bag of cashews and a Nalgine container filled with brandy) and dinner was served (corn on the cob, sourdough bread, fried dale mushrooms, steaks as thick as dictionaries and, of course, a cake). Then the threesome gathered around the evening fire and told Scott and me hair-raising stories of previous trips on the Dumoine, when the water was colder and the rapids were wilder. Needless to say, their reminiscing did little to ease our apprehension, and I ended up popping another anti-nausea pill before going off to bed.

The next morning, in what seemed like no time at all, the first rapids appeared ahead. We ran two quick swifts back-to-back and then, after eddying in on the left, Scott and I looked down at the humped-up waves and white froth of what was considered to be only a Class I rapid. We immediately declined to go first and invited the others to go ahead of us. Len and Roy went center and then right. Rick, in his fancy solo boat, hugged the right bank all the way down. Then Scott and I bumped and grinded our way straight down the center, leaving behind canoe paint on the rocks like bread crumbs on a forest trail.

Embarrassed about our blunder, Scott and I insisted we act as probes for the next rapid. We approached the drop slowly, with me standing up in the stern half-a-dozen times to choose the proper channel. "Just keep right!" I yelled, and away we went, bouncing through the largest of the standing waves but avoiding the entire collection of jagged rocks sticking out in midstream.

We maneuvered through one more Class I rapid before taking out on the portage for Ragged Chutes. The 1,640-yard (1,500 m) rough trail — called Grunt Portage — is on the left bank and avoids three large and totally unnavigable chutes. No mistaking it, the portage does live up to its nickname. However, a low-water take-out directly before the first drop and a number of side trails that allow experienced canoeists to paddle some quiet stretches in between can reduce the carry to only 352 yards (322 m).

Soon after the "triple play" is Bridge Rapids — a good Class II followed directly by three easy Class Is (but that's if the water level is well above the rocks). Before heading down this fun stretch of rapids, however, our gang was hailed to shore by a group of canoeists camped to the right of the decrepit bridge. They had somehow driven a trailer of canoes in by way of an extremely rough dirt road and along the way managed to drag a fiberglass Prospector behind them for over twenty minutes. By the looks of it, their trip was over before it started. But we gave them a spare roll of duct tape just the same and then continued on our way.

Once past Lac Benoit (a popular fly-in point for a three- to four-day trip) a technical Class I warms things up for what's next — a Class II directly above a dangerous falls. A rough 33-yard (30 m) portage is on the right of the Class II. But Scott and I kept upright by staying away from the big standing waves to the left and then managed to eddy in just before the 77-yard (70 m) portage marked to the right of the falls.

Canoe Eater, a very technical Class III waiting not far downstream, is a different story, however. The entire run is difficult to scout from shore and a nasty rock garden blocks the upper section. So Scott and I opted for the 250-yard

(225 m) portage to the right. Of course, after we saw Len, Roy and Rick all being spit out at the bottom, we knew we had made the right choice.

Remarkably enough, another group of canoeists headed blindly down Canoe Eater on the tail end of Len and Roy. Why their actions bothered me so much was that neither of them wore, nor even owned, a lifejacket. As well, by watching how they kept their paddles high and dry while plowing through the haystacks at the bottom, I knew they lacked any experience paddling in technical rapids.

We were all concerned about the novice paddlers, but Roy and Rick are both paramedics and couldn't live with themselves if they allowed the group to continue on without saying something. But after a polite chat and a generous offer to help them navigate the rest of the river, both Rick and Roy were told to go straight to hell. I couldn't believe it. In all my years of paddling, I've never witnessed idiots like these — and I hope I never will again.

We took on seven more runs before making camp at a site called the Hobbit (a place rumored to hold evil spirits living inside the cliff face). The first and last rapid were shallow Class Is, and the middle five (the Sleeper, Double Choice, the Snake, Thread the Needle, and Log Jam Rapids) were all technical Class IIs.

Scott and I blew the third Class II. The rapid twists its way from left to right and then left again, but just after the initial drop a side-curler shoved our boat out of the main channel. Scott leaned over to try to draw the bow straight, and just then a splash of water almost filled the canoe. We were completely out of control. All we could do was to ride it out, bracing and reacting as we went, and somehow we managed to stay afloat until the bitter end.

Now spooked from that run, my partner and I took a rough 130-yard (120 m) portage to the right of Thread the Needle. It's a scary run, and if you mess up you could easily find your canoe pinned on the center boulder near the bottom. True to form, the others managed the rapid with no problem and then waited patiently for Scott and me to drag our soggy packs and 86-pound Old Town Tripper through the bush. We were rewarded at the end, however, by witnessing the bozos we had met upstream swimming down the rapids, without the aid of lifejackets.

The next morning we awoke to the rumbling sounds of Little Steel Rapids, situated only a few hundred yards downstream from our "Hobbit" campsite. Scott and I, feeling more courageous than the days before, led the way to the brink of the long stretch of boiling water. We flushed our way down the first drop (an easy Class II) and then eddied in on the left to peer down at what was next. Still confident, I stood up and scouted the best route through the remaining Class IIs. (A 77-yard [70 m] portage on the right can be used to avoid the worst part of Little Steel Rapids.) After okaying my choice with my partner, we abandoned our eddy by ferrying upstream and then leaned into the current, keeping to the right channel, and committed ourselves to the whitewater waiting below. It was a perfect run and Scott and I finally had our confidence back.

Little Steel Falls, almost directly after Little Steel Rapids, was a prime objective for Len, Roy and Rick. A few years back, during extremely high water levels,

Dumoine River

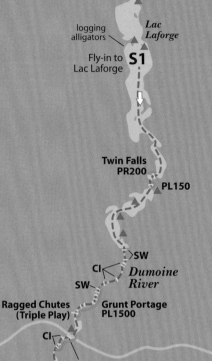

logging
alligators

*Lac
Laforge*

Fly-in to
Lac Laforge **S1**

Twin Falls
PR200

PL150

SW

CI

*Dumoine
River*

SW

**Ragged Chutes
(Triple Play)**

**Grunt Portage
PL1500**

CI

Bridge Rapids PL400 CII
(rapids under bridge)

*Lac
Benoit*

Fly-in to
Lac Benoit **S2**

CI

PR30

CII

falls PR70

Canoe Eater CIII

PR225

CI

The Snake CII

The Sleeper CII

Thread the Needle CII

Double Choice CII

PR120

Gooseneck Rapids CI

Hobbit Campsite

Log Jam Rapids CII

CI-II

Little Steel Rapids
(see inset)

Little Steel Falls

PR312

CII-III
alt. PL280

CI

CII

SW

Scenic Chute

SW

Cliff Hanger CII

old logslide

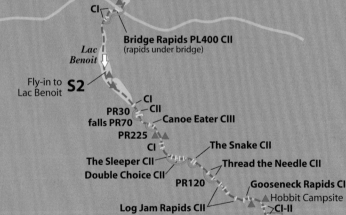

S	start
F	finish: two options
⌒	portage
PL50	portage left 50 meters
PR60	portage right 60 meters
SW	swift
- - -	route
•••••	alternate route
———	road
∿	rapid, falls
▨	park boundary
▲	campsite
⟹	direction of travel

ledge

CII-III

CII

CII-III

PR70

CII

**Little
Steel
Rapids**

**Note: Only rough trails
exist where no portages
are marked**

0 km 1

0 mi 1

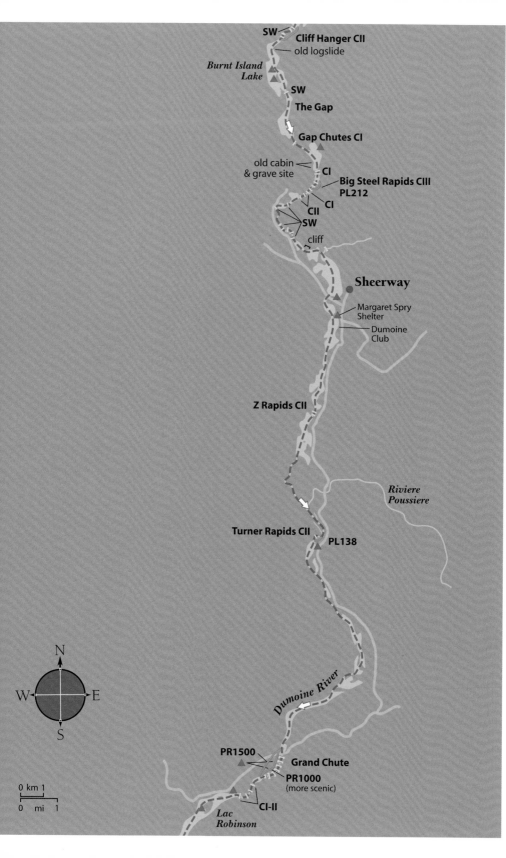

SW
Cliff Hanger CII
old logslide

Burnt Island Lake

SW

The Gap

Gap Chutes CI

old cabin
& grave site
CI
Big Steel Rapids CIII
PL212
CI
CII
SW
cliff

Sheerway

Margaret Spry
Shelter
Dumoine
Club

Z Rapids CII

*Riviere
Poussiere*

Turner Rapids CII
PL138

Dumoine River

PR1500

Grand Chute
PR1000
(more scenic)

CI-II

*Lac
Robinson*

N
W   E
S

0 km 1
0 mi 1

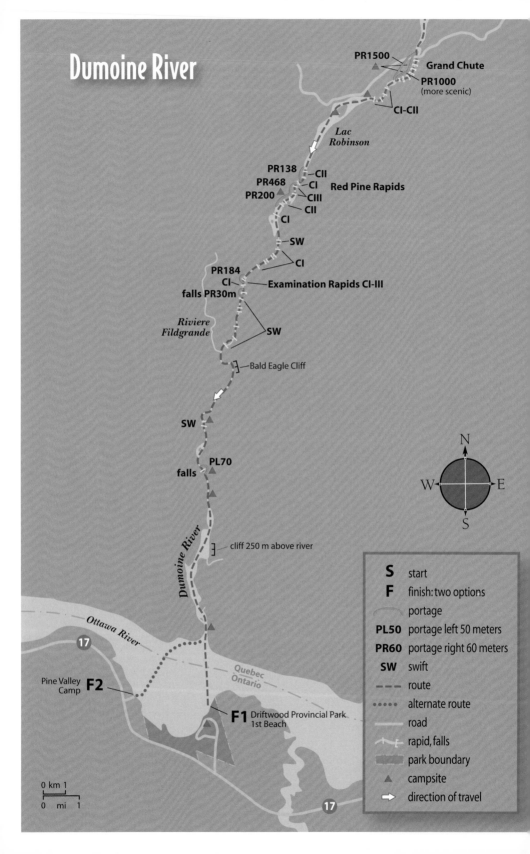

Dumoine River

PR1500
Grand Chute
PR1000
(more scenic)
CI-CII

Lac Robinson

PR138 — CII
PR468 — CI **Red Pine Rapids**
PR200 — CIII
— CII
— CI

— SW
— CI

PR184
CI — **Examination Rapids CI-III**
falls PR30m

Riviere Fildgrande
— SW

— Bald Eagle Cliff

SW

PL70
falls

cliff 250 m above river

Dumoine River

Ottawa River
17

Quebec
Ontario

Pine Valley Camp **F2**

F1 Driftwood Provincial Park
1st Beach

N
W — E
S

S	start
F	finish: two options
⌒	portage
PL50	portage left 50 meters
PR60	portage right 60 meters
SW	swift
- - -	route
••••	alternate route
⸺	road
⊢⊣	rapid, falls
▨	park boundary
▲	campsite
➡	direction of travel

0 km 1
0 mi 1

17

Roy had attempted to run the boiling water below the cascade and dumped almost immediately. Except for a long cold swim, Len and Rick figured Roy would be fine, and they calmly worked their way down to the base of the rapids to toss out a throwbag. When they reached the end of the whitewater, however, only Roy's canoe, paddle and favorite hat were floating in the quiet water. Unknown to them, their partner was being held underwater by a one-piece rainsuit filled with water. Miraculously, Roy was able to slice open the rubber overalls with his belt knife and he finally found his way to the surface and grabbed the safety line.

To be honest, I would've stayed clear of the rapids below Little Steel Falls if the same thing had happened to me. Not Roy — he was determined to make things right. So while the rest of us carried over the full length of the 340-yard (312 m) portage, found along the right bank (an alternate 400-yard [306 m] portage is also marked on the left), Roy just lifted over the first 55 yards (50 m), plopped his plastic boat into a pool below the falls and then finessed his way through the series of Class IIs and Class IIIs. We all applauded him from the safety of the portage and then ceremoniously threw him the safety line as he ended the run still afloat.

Not far downstream from Little Steel Falls is a Class I and then a voluminous Class II, followed by a number of fun swifts. Then the river widens out. Our group thought of stopping for a break on a rocky point to the left, until we discovered the campsite was only suitable for mountain goats. So we continued, running Cliff Hanger — a Class II known for its steep rock wall towering high above the base of the rapids — and then pulled up on an island campsite in the middle of Burnt Island Lake.

The forested hills here were impressive — appearing to be trackless and impenetrable. This wasn't the first scenic spot along the Dumoine. In fact, the entire river seemed to be surrounded by pinnacles of rock. But so far the motion of the river had kept the scenery concealed. Now, taking time out to look at the rugged landscape, I found myself appreciating the beauty of places like Burnt Island Lake even more than the thrill of the rapids.

A small swift separates Burnt Island Lake and another widening in the river called the Gap. Then comes Gap Chutes — a Class I where lots of water squeezes you to the far right — followed by an easy Class I. (The rustic remains of an old cabin and a wooden cross marking the grave of a victim of the river can be found on the west shore, just before the rapids.)

As with Little Steel Rapids, we heard Big Steel Rapids well before we saw it. There's a 232-yard (212 m) portage to the left that avoids a challenging Class III at the beginning. But Len, Roy and Rick convinced Scott and me that there was just a bit of water to contend with. So we followed them over the brink and somehow managed to stay afloat through the biggest standing waves of the trip. Proud of our achievements we paddled hard toward the next set — a technical Class II. Two obvious channels lay before us — a wide one to the far left and a tight turn to the right. We decided to go left, and began

The biggest advantage of choosing to run rapids rather than carry over lengthy portages is that you get to pack along more food!

ferrying across toward the channel. Halfway, however, we collided with a rock at a 30-degree angle. The boat just about went over, but a quick downstream lean pivoted us around the obstacle and we stayed dry.

Shortly after Big Steel was a collection of swifts that took us past cobble beaches and high sandy banks, and then ended at an impressively high cliff. It was a totally different environment than the rest of the Dumoine, reminding me more of the rivers that flowed into Ontario's Lake Superior than Quebec's Ottawa Valley, but I enjoyed it immensely.

We soon paddled by Sheerway (an active farmstead at the turn of the century), passed under a bridge, and then made camp at what's called the Margaret Spry Shelter. The lean-to structure was built by the Dumoine Rod and Gun Club, who have made use of the log house across the river since 1918.

Here we had another birthday celebration; this time for Len's eighty-year-old mother. Obviously she wasn't with us on the trip, but it seemed like a great excuse to bake another cake and drink some more brandy. And since Len was missing the festivities back home (his mother insisted he join us canoeing instead), we forced him to wear a T-shirt around camp that read Happy Birthday, Mom.

A good part of day four was spent paddling leisurely down the quiet stretch before Grand Chute, where there are only two Class IIs, Z Rapids and Turner Rapids, to contend with. On the first run, Scott and I took the left channel, grabbed an eddy behind a giant boulder to avoid being pushed into a rock garden, and then exited to the right. The second was more challenging and it had an optional 150-yard (138 m) portage located well before the rapid, along the left bank. By using the portage you can avoid the most difficult section, but Scott and I simply couldn't find the path and we took on the entire run. Believe me, you're going to get wet on this one!

To carry around Grand Chute you have two portages to chose from, both of which begin on the right side of the river. The scenic route, complete with a campsite overlooking the gorge, is straight across from the take-out and follows alongside the entire drop for 1,100 yards (1,000 m). To take the alternate route, measuring 1,640 yards (1,500 m), keep to the road until a marked trail heads into the woods to your left. The shorter path is okay if you're loaded with packs. But if you happen to be stuck carrying the canoe, I strongly suggest heading up the road. You may not see much of Grand Chute along the way, but you do have a canoe over your head.

It started to rain on us after we completed the Grand Chute portage and the downpour worsened as we crossed Lac Robinson. So the group decided to make camp at a nice site located halfway down Red Pine Rapids, directly under a massive pine tree.

As we drifted above the first drop on Red Pine, however, disaster struck. A hailstorm came barreling down the river like a freight train, catching us completely off guard. We all scattered, Scott and I making it over to the left bank to a patch of low-hanging cedars, Rick to the take-out for the 150-yard (138 m) portage on the right bank. Len and Roy, already committed to the running the rapids when the storm hit, went over the first ledge and quickly dropped out of sight

It was a good twenty minutes before the storm died down enough for us to head back out on the river again. Worried about Len and Roy, we skipped the portage and flushed ourselves directly down the first and second ledges. In retrospect, it was an extremely difficult Class II that we paddled through, but Scott and I were thinking more about Len and Roy than the power of the river. They were safe, though, and were standing at the take-out of a second portage that avoids a dangerous Class III. Chilled from the rain, we all decided to take the

510-yard (468 m) portage, marked to the right, and made camp under the pine tree. Here, celebrating our last night on the Dumoine, we baked another cake — a double-decker with jam in the middle and topped with icing, blueberries and shredded chocolate — and then toasted the river with the remaining brandy.

In the morning, a little groggy from too much dessert (and possibly too much liquor), the group was slow to start. It was 9:30 a.m. before we were packed up and started looking for a way to deal with what remained of Red Pine Rapids. It was a rocky Class II, with a ledge extending far out from our side of the river. A rough 220-yard (200 m) path continuing down from our campsite avoided the entire mess, but none of us wanted to wimp out on the first rapid of the day. So by ferrying across to the opposite bank we were all able to make use of an obvious channel that stayed clear of the ledge and then we picked our way through the mound of rocks below.

Next we easily paddled our way down a combination of swifts and three easy Class Is. But when our group approached a double-ledged Class II called Examination Rapids — the last difficult rapid on the Dumoine — we all pulled up at the take-out for the 200-yard (184 m) portage on the right and had a good look.

The first drop didn't seem to be a problem. The difficulty would be in actually staying dry after coming through it and then lining up perfectly for the last drop. With a souse hole to the left and a jumble of rocks to the right, there was no margin for error.

After watching the others make perfect runs, Scott and I decided to give it a try. Nervously we launched ourselves out into the river, and right away noted how much bigger it all looks closer up.

Of course we ran into trouble right away. Being more concerned about what lay ahead, Scott and I hit the first ledge completely wrong, took on water, and then found ourselves heading sideways directly toward the giant funnel of water. "Right! Right!" I screamed. But Scott's repeated draw strokes did nothing to pivot us back into position. It wasn't until just before the curling water gulped us down that I realized our mistake. It was me. I was so uptight about what Scott was doing up in the bow that I failed to do my job in the stern. So, with a strong pry, I cranked the back end of the canoe around and we hit the smooth wide tongue we had planned on reaching, and then rode the edge of the waves all the way to the bottom.

"Nice recovery" was all we got from the three onlookers, each of them standing on shore with a safety line in hand. But Scott and I whooped it up like a couple of ecstatic schoolboys, spun our paddles over our heads, and then whooped it up some more. Finally they all laughed and then applauded our fancy maneuvers.

Just downstream from Examination Rapids a small Class I warns you of an approaching falls; avoid the falls with a 33-yard (30 m) portage on the right. Then, after some continuous swifts before the junction of the Fildegrand River, a breathtaking 590-foot-high (180 m) rock face called Bald Eagle Cliff, and another scenic falls with a quick 77-yard (70 m) portage marked to the left, comes the nerve-wracking paddle across the expanse of the Ottawa River.

Luckily the river was calm when we made the crossing. For me, it was one of the most relaxed times of the entire trip. That is, until we reached the other side. It was here that I had to tell the others that I forgot to ask our shuttle driver where exactly at Driftwood Provincial Park he was going to leave our vehicle. Let's just say that by the time we found it, parked up the hill from the first beach, I was looking through my pockets for another anti-nausea pill.

The Dumoine River

TIME 4 to 5 days

DIFFICULTY Moderate to advanced, due to lack of portages around many Class I, Class II and even Class III rapids.

PORTAGES 15

LONGEST PORTAGE 1,640 yards (1,500 m)

BEST TIME TO RUN IT Spring through fall

FEE The fly-in is a must, but Bradley Air Service's price is quite reasonable.

ALTERNATIVE ROUTE Trips can be lengthened by one or two days by flying into Lac Dumoine or Lac Sept Milles and shortened to a long weekend by flying into Lac Benoit.

OUTFITTERS
Bradley Air Service
Box 3
Rapides Des Joachims, Quebec
K0J 2H0
613-586-2374
or
613-432-3471

Valley Ventures
Box 1115
Deep River, Ontario
K0J 1P0
613-584-2577
www.magma.ca

Tuckamore Trips Inc.
7123 Lac Noir Road
Ste-Agathe-des-Monts, Quebec
J8C 2Z8
819-326-3602

FOR MORE INFORMATION
Federation Quebecoise du canot-camping inc.
4545, av. Pierre-Des Coubertin
C.P. 1000, Succ. N.
Montreal, Quebec
H1V 3R2
514-252-3001
www.canot-kayak.qc.ca

MAPS The Federation Quebecoise du-canot-camping has produced a pamphlet on the Dumoine River. Hap Wilson's guidebook, *Rivers of the Upper Ottawa Valley: Myth, Magic and Adventure*, is also an excellent resource.

TOPOGRAPHIC MAPS 31 K/13, 31 K/12, 31 K/5 & 31 K/4

Not all canoes make it down the wild waters of the Dumoine River.

A Weekend on the Coulonge

IN 1984, WHEN E. B. EDDY DISCONTINUED ITS LAKE POMPONNE CAMP, the Coulonge became the last tributary of the Ottawa River to witness the log drives. The blemish still remains, with lost timber continuously washing up on banks, jamming in rock cuts and littering back bays. But recently, the river has shown signs of a comeback and is quickly becoming one of Quebec's prime canoe routes.

The total length of the Coulonge is 167 miles (270 km), allowing for an extensive two-week venture if you're up to it. But it's the last stretch — a two-to-three-day jaunt down from Lac Jim — that provides the most fun. In fact, with prime sand beaches for camping, lots of calm stretches where you can relax and let the current carry you downstream, and plenty of ledge-type descents to challenge even the most advanced paddler, it's surprising that the river is seldom busy — especially during the fall season.

When I first paddled the river, in 1997 — joined then by Robin Rivison, his teenage son, Glenn, and one of my regular canoe partners, Scott Roberts — we left a second vehicle at Grand Chute Conservation Area. It can be reached by turning north off Highway 148 onto Bois France Road, east of the town of Fort Coulonge. At present, however, this is discouraged by the staff and you're best to park beside a bridge not far upstream. To park here, take the Golf Course Road just before the conservation area. The golf course itself is also a possible take-out point if you're worried about leaving your car at the bridge.

To access the river, take Lac Jim Road, located back out along Bois France Road, toward the highway. Then, just past Kilometer 36 (marked by a small blue metal sign), turn right onto Lac Galarneau Road and put in to the right of the bridge joining Lac Galarneau and Lac Jim. Or, if your vehicle can handle backroad driving, continue driving straight to the river and put in below Rapids Enrages. Again, if you're uncomfortable about leaving your car unattended, you could use Lac Jim Paradise Lodge, which is reached by a half-mile-long dirt road just before Lac Galarneau Road.

To reach the river from Lac Jim, paddle across to its weedy northeastern bay and take the 137-yard (125 m) portage to the left of the concrete dam. For the first few miles, the river doesn't have much in the way of difficult whitewater, just a total of nine swifts before where the East Branch joins in with the Coulonge on the left, two more directly afterward, and then a triple set collectively called Poplar Rapids. Later on, however, a Class II needs some attention. There's a dirt path on the right that acts as a good portage — measuring 275 yards (250 m) — but a sign reading Chien de Garde (Guard Dog) is posted near a cabin at the end of the path. The moment our group saw the sign, we turned

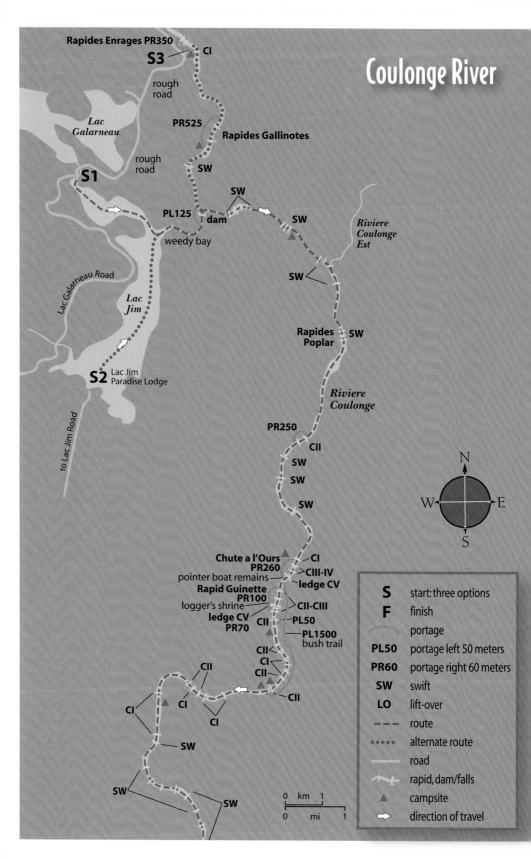

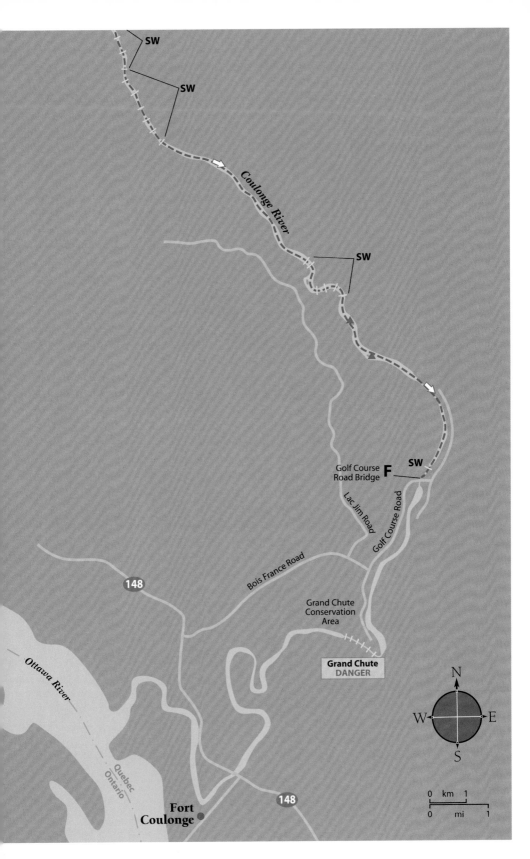

Poplar Rapids, Coulonge River. The dog, Sadie, prefers to portage.

tail and ran the entire set, keeping to the center until the end. There Robin and Glenn took the left channel and got a lap-full of water after punching through a large standing wave, and Scott and I chickened out by scraping through a boulder garden to the right.

Next, after three more swifts, is Chute à l'Ours. We made camp here, close to the take-out for the 286-yard (260 m) portage on the right. But first we ran down the initial drop — a Class I rapid — and then quickly eddied in alongside a beach on the west bank. The campsite is just up from the beach, high up on a heap of rock. This is the same site that author and canoeist Tony Sloan mentions in his book *Blackflies and White Water* (1977) as the "tent town" where a group of river drivers stayed while working downriver. "The forty-man crew ranged from relative youngsters in their teens, lean, long-haired and shirtless, to older, heavy-bodied veterans, whose close-cropped and greying hair indicated most of a lifetime spent on drives through the chutes and rapids of the Coulonge."

At the end of the 286-yard (260 m) portage you'll see the remains of a pointer boat, confirming Sloan's story; he says it was either rowed by a dozen or more men or powered by a large outboard motor.

Not far downstream from Chute à l'Ours is an even larger drop called Rapid Guinette. Here, Sloan's book makes reference to a lengthy portage running well over a kilometer (over half a mile) along the left bank. Our group took some time out to try to locate the old bush trail but had little luck, which was fine with us, since the author calls it "a goddamn hike!" So, much as with the previous chute, we ran a Class I to the right, and then immediately eddied in against the west bank. From here we walked down a rugged, almost nonexistent bush trail, to scout a tight Class II just before the main chute. All four of us took some time peering down at the funnel of water to evaluate the possibilities, giving special attention to where a curling wave could quite easily heave a canoe unexpectedly toward a giant boulder. Then we returned to the boats to give it a try.

Robin and Glenn were first, and except for coming down hard on the last bit, theirs was a dry run. Scott and I, even though we managed to take the darkest V in the rapid and come out of the standing waves still upright, somehow banged into a rock broadside at the end. The river quickly began pouring in. Luckily, we were able to pull in behind the next boulder and dragged ourselves safely to shore.

Directly after the Class II there's a 77-yard (70 m) portage that avoids a sharp ledge. (Look for the wooden marker commemorating riverman Alex Guinette, who drowned in the rapids some years ago.) A good Class II or Class III (depending on water levels) continues soon after the main drop, and you either have to run through it all or lift over a rock outcrop on the far right. In each case, however, you're left with a triple ledge to contend with before the rapids end. They're not too difficult, as long as you line up properly and take it slowly. But a 55-yard (50 m) bush trail on the left can be used to avoid all three.

After a short calm stretch the current quickens again, and for the next 3 miles (5 km) we rode the most enjoyable stretch of whitewater, made up of moderately challenging Class II rapids and short choppy Class I curls, where we had little to do except ride along and revel in it.

What remains is a river of a placid nature, a slim thread winding through rural woods and cow pastures, with half a dozen swifts to break up the lazy paddle to the bridge take-out. But well before reaching this calm stretch — in fact, about a quarter of the way down the long set of rapids below Rapid Guinette — our group made camp for our last night. There was a choice of two sites on the right bank; one pushed back into the woods and the other out in the middle of a sandbar. We took the more exposed site, hoping for a steady breeze to keep down the no-see-ums —miniature biting insects notorious for hanging around sandy points. And, for our traditional last-night dinner, the group baked a cake to be washed down later with hot chocolate spiced with Bailey's Irish Cream.

A Weekend on the Coulonge

TIME 2 to 3 days

DIFFICULTY Most rapids cannot be portaged, so you should have at least moderate whitewater skills.

PORTAGES 5

LONGEST PORTAGE
286 yards (260 m)

BEST TIME TO RUN IT The Coulonge holds its water well throughout the season but the fall is best.

FEE The route travels through Crown land, where no fee is required for Canadian citizens. A moderate fee is required if you decide to park at Lac Jim Paradise Lodge or have your vehicle shuttled.

ALTERNATIVE ROUTE If your vehicle can handle backroad driving, then head directly to the river, below Rapids Enrages, by continuing along Lac Galarneau Road. From here to the Lac Jim dam, you'll have a Class II to run and a 574-yard (525 m) portage to take to the right of Rapides Gallinotes.

OUTFITTERS
Noire & Coulonge River Expeditions (Michel Pouliot)
23 Joanisse Street, Apt. 4
Hull, Quebec
J8X I84
819-778-6347

Valley Ventures
Box 1115,
Deep River, Ontario
K0J 1P0
613-584-2577

Tuckamor Trips Inc.
7123 Lac Noir Road,
Ste-Agathe-des-Monts, Quebec
J8C 2Z8
819-326-3602

Eco-Yote
Highway 148
Mansfield/Fort Coulonge
C.P. 1288
Quebec
819-683-3150

FOR MORE INFORMATION
Federation Quebecoise du canot-camping inc.
4545, av. Pierre-De Coubertin
C.P. 1000, Succ. N
H1V 3R2
Montreal, Quebec
514-252-3001
www.canot-kayak.qc.ca

MAPS The Federation Quebecoise du canot-camping has produced a pamphlet on the Coulonge (in French only). Hap Wilson's guide-book, *The Rivers of the Ottawa Valley: Myth, Magic and Adventure*, is also an excellent resource.

TOPOGRAPHIC MAPS
31 K/02 & 31 K/15

La Verendrye's Chochocouane River

SOME PEOPLE HAVE CALLED LA VERENDRYE WILDLIFE RESERVE Quebec's Algonquin. At first, the comparison seems quite reasonable: the reserve has over 4,000 lakes and rivers and a network of canoe routes totaling 1,365 miles (2,200 km). There's one slight difference, though. Algonquin receives an average of 200,000 visitors per season and La Verendrye peaks at a mere 5,000. That's what makes the Chochocouane River — situated in the northeast end of La Verendrye, one of the more remote sections of the reserve — an exceptional canoe route. You're almost guaranteed to have the place to yourself, something Algonquin could never offer.

It is possible to paddle a five-day or even an extensive eight-day loop, starting and ending at Lac Elbow and making use of the Canimiti, Denain and Chochocouane Rivers. But the Canimiti rarely has enough water to make for a pleasant trip throughout the season and most canoeists find it best to just organize a car shuttle and paddle the Chochocouane from top to bottom.

Before beginning the river you first must pick up a camping permit at La Verendrye's Canoe Camping office in Le Domaine, located on the west side of Highway 117, about a quarter the way through the reserve. Shuttles can also be arranged through the permit office; the gravel road leading to the put-in is a long and bumpy one, so it may be best to pay a staff member instead of playing chicken with the local logging trucks.

The take-out is located 53 miles (86 km) north of Le Domaine at Camping des Outaouais. The parking area is marked to the left, halfway across the Dozois Reservoir bridge. From here it's another 36 miles (58 km) to Chimo Road, where you turn right just before the Felix River. There are a number of side roads off Chimo Road, but by keeping to the main gravel section you should be fine. Almost 40 miles (63 km but marked on blue road-signs as Kilometer 102), there's a major fork in the road. Canoeists looking for a five-day paddle down the Chochocouane should bear to the right and use the put-in to the left of the iron bridge, just above a moderate Class I rapid. For a six-day trip, keep to the main road and put in 9 miles (15 km) upstream, at the outlet of Lac Douai.

I've tried both access points and find the extra day not worth the effort, especially because the main logging road runs parallel with the river. Even that 5-mile (8 km) stretch downstream from the first access point is spoiled enough with the sounds of trucks hauling out logs; you're well-advised to escape the upper reaches of the Chochocouane as soon as possible.

About 6 miles (10 km) downriver from the five-day put-in are the remains of a Native camp. Abandoned not long ago, it looks like a garbage heap at first glance. But among the discarded clothes and food tins are beaver skulls and wooden hoops used to stretch out pelts, attesting to the more traditional side of life that still exists in northern Quebec.

A little more than a mile (2 km) beyond the former Native camp is the first major stretch of fast water, beginning with a sharp drop and a mixture of Class II and Class III rapids. Experienced paddlers may want to chance this one, but it's probably wise to make use of the easy 148-yard (135 m) portage marked to the right.

Almost immediately after is a even more difficult run where a 27-yard (25 m) portage is marked to the left of a ledge and then continues on for another 345 yards (315 m) around two technical Class IIs. The first has a tight V on the far right and the second has a sharp corner at the end that you must maneuver around with care to avoid slamming into a rock wall. Running the ledge is obviously out of the question, but I would seriously consider running the rapids below rather than carry over the rugged portage, which has a steep bank just before the put-in.

A runnable Class II and a quick stretch of fast water soon follow, but after that it's a long arduous paddle through a forest of regenerated spruce and jack pine. Here you stand a good chance of spotting a moose and an even better chance at hearing a wolf howl come nightfall, especially in late August and September when the over-zealous cubs will bark out at the drop of a hat.

Grand Chute, Chochocouane River.

A 252-yard (230 m) portage is marked to the right of the next set of rapids. It's relatively flat and ends at a great beach campsite. But most of the lower half has been taken over by a thick alder patch, and running the rapid — a technical Class II in low water and an advanced Class III in high water — is a much better choice as long as your skills are up to snuff.

A quick Class I finishes off the run, with an even more overgrown 137-yard (125 m) portage to the right. Then, not far downstream is a Class III with an easy 104-yard (95 m) portage to the right, followed by a Class II that must be run since its lacks any signs of a true portage.

Except for the odd swift formed between a jumble of rocks and where the soft current comes out of Lac Gustave, the river remains quite calm right up until a place called Island Cascades. I find this location extremely confusing. The park map clearly shows two distinct channels to the left and right of an island but in reality only the one to the left seems to exist. Of course, that makes the take-out for the so-called island portage difficult to spot. And, to make matters worse, the 94-yard (85 m) trail has a network of side routes leading to a lookout for the Class IV chute on the left, a group campsite near the put-in, and an outhouse somewhere in between.

Two more Class II rapids follow in quick succession, one immediately after the island portage and the other about a ten-minute paddle downstream. The first has no portage. But the second has a 71-yard (65 m) trail to the right. It's hardly used, though, and again, running the rapids seem easier than bushwhacking through alder thickets.

A cross also stands near the base of the second rapid, on the north bank. It's unmarked, but a miniature pointer-boat carved from wood and nailed to the base of the cross, which is decorated with plastic flowers and a statue of Jesus, gives some evidence that it's a logger's grave site.

Remnants of a logging bridge 2.5 miles (4 km) downstream mark the whereabouts of the next set of rapids — another easy Class II and Class I with no portage — as well as the place where the Denain River joins the Chochocoune. Then, an hour-and-a-half paddle brings you to one of the most scenic spots en route — Grand Chute. You have a choice of portages here; a 190-yard (175 m) trail on the left or a 230-yard (210 m) portage on the right. Other than that they're 38 yards (35 m) apart and the trail on the right has a designated campsite at the take-out, they're identical; why we're even given the choice is a mystery.

Three more sets come between Grand Chute and the confluence of the Canimiti River. The first is a simple Class I that can be run either in the center or to the far right. The second is a huge Class V that, obviously, must be portaged 60 yards (55 m) on the left. And the third is a long, challenging set, the major problem being a Class III directly after the first drop. (A 660-yard [600 m] portage on the right can be used to avoid this set.)

Only two more major drops remain before the river is mixed in with the stale waters of the Dozois Reservoir. The first is a technical Class II that can be

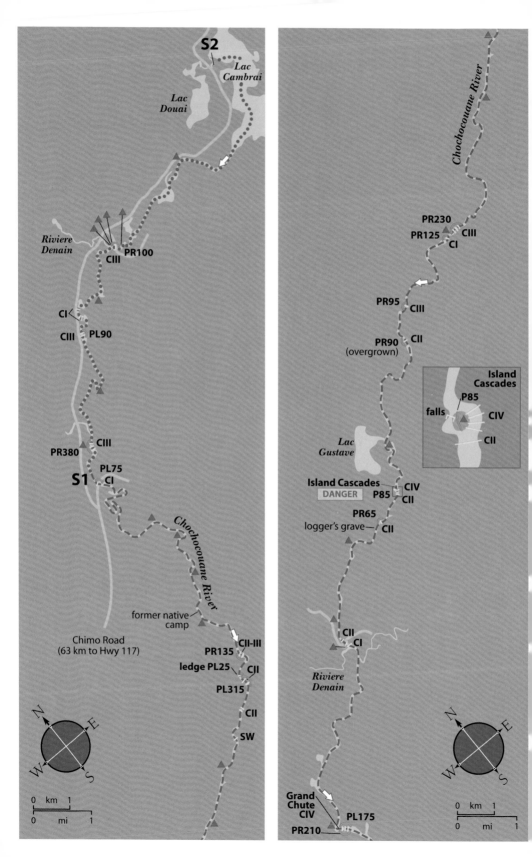

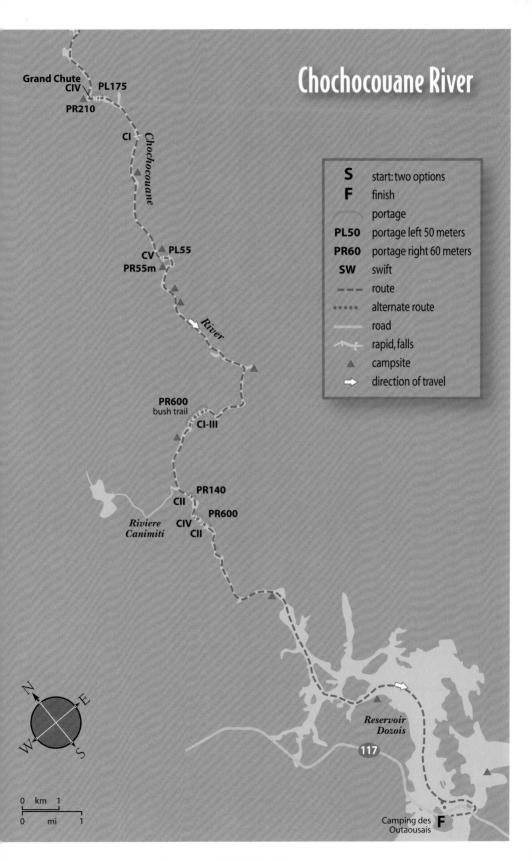

"Are we there yet?" Christine, Helen and I take a side trip up the Canimiti River.

run or portaged 153 yards (140 m) on the left. Next is a collection of chutes that supposedly disappear when the reservoir is high and become the worst obstacle on the river if the water is low; and you guessed it — the water is usually low. So, either make use of an overgrown 660-yard (600 m) portage along the left bank (the take-out is found just before a large boulder) or lift over on the rocks beside the first chute and hope to stay afloat in the foam and froth that remains.

After the final drop, it's a simple case of flushing yourself down a few swifts and then making sure you keep to the main channel that will eventually lead you out into the reservoir and toward the take-out on the west side of Highway 117. Sounds easy, but when some canoe mates, Christine Neff and Helen Penny, and I paddled the river last year, we found ourselves lost twice in the maze of rotten stumps and dead-end inlets. By the time we reached the main section of the reservoir, the winds had started to pick up. Trust me. You definitely don't want to find yourself windbound on the Dozois Reservoir. It's a complete wasteland. In fact, we were so eager to end our paddle here that, rather than use the bridge 1.25 miles (2 km) to the south, the safe way to reach the take-out on the opposite side of the highway, Christine, Helen and I chose to dodge the traffic and cross over while loaded down with packs and canoes. It was an insane move but it was worth it to rid ourselves of the manmade eyesore and end our trip still in good spirits.

La Verendrye's Chochocouane River

TIME 5 to 6 days

DIFFICULTY This is an excellent river for whitewater enthusiasts with moderate skills.

PORTAGES 12

LONGEST PORTAGE
660 yards (600 m)

BEST TIME TO RUN IT Spring through fall (but water level changes dramatically due to control dam)

FEE An interior camping permit must be purchased at La Verendrye's Canoe Camping office in Le Domaine, located on the west side of Highway 117, about a quarter of the way through the reserve. And there is the possible cost of shuttle service.

ALTERNATIVE ROUTE A five- or even eight-day loop can be made in the earlier part of the season, starting and ending at the Lac Elbow access point, east of Highway 117, by making use of the Canimiti and Chochocouane Rivers.

OUTFITTERS
La Verendrye Canoe Camping
Base le Domaine
819-435-2331

FOR MORE INFORMATION
**Federation Quebecoise du canot-
    camping inc.**
4545, av. Pierre-De Coubertin
C.P. 1000, Succ. M,
H1V 3R2
Montreal, Quebec
H1V 3R2
514-252-3001
www.canot-kayak.qc.ca

MAPS La Verendrye Canoe Camping has produced an excellent canoe map.

TOPOGRAPHIC MAPS
31 N/11, 31 N/14 & 31 N/15
Special note: at the time of this writing, no dogs are allowed in La Verendrye Reserve.

The Desert River

IT WAS WHILE SURFING THE WEB LATE ONE EVENING that I first learned of the Desert River that flows out of Quebec's ZEC Bras-Coupe Desert (819-449-3838) — a 465-square-mile (1,200 sq km) reserve situated just south of La Verendrye. The information was quite vague, telling only that the name of the river may have originated from the great number of sand beaches found along its banks. But the promise of two to three days basking in sun and sand was all I needed to convince my beach-bum friends Mike Cullen, Jeff Taylor and his brother Greg to join me on what we found to be one of the best unsung routes western Quebec has to offer.

The river itself ends in the town of Maniwaki, where it empties out into the Gatineau River. But the best take-out is 19 miles (30 km) upstream at a bridge just outside Montcerf. To reach the small hamlet and drop a second vehicle off, drive north of Maniwaki on Highway 105, and just after Bois-Franc make a left. It's almost 4 miles (6 km) to Montcerf. You can either park your vehicle near the bridge or store it in the church parking lot up the road. If you choose the church, just ask for permission first — and drop a few dollars in the collection plate while you're at it.

From Montcerf, you can either drive back to Highway 105 the same way you came or take the 10.5-mile (17 km) side road heading north out of town. In each case you make a left at Highway 105 and then, just past the gas station at the bottom of the hill, turn left again onto the road leading into ZEC Bras-Coupe Desert. (If you enter La Verendrye Reserve, you've gone too far.)

Stop at the gatehouse and pay the moderate fee for camping over for the first half of the trip in the reserve, then drive 12 miles (19 km) to the Lac du Pont access point. The parking area is on the far side of the bridge and to the left of the roadway. If you're arriving late on a Friday night you can either set up camp just north of the bridge or, in an hour's time, paddle the weedy outlet leading to Lac Rond and make camp on a prime beach site marked along the east shore.

The Desert River drains out of Lac Rond at the northeast end. Soon after, a small bridge marks the whereabouts of the first rapids en route. The top section, just before the bridge, is a Class II, probably because there's a good chance of hitting the metal bars holding the bridge up. The bottom half is an easy Class I, however. So either use the entire 66-yard (60 m) portage on the left or simply carry around the bridge and paddle through what's left.

Just around the next bend is Island Rapids. There's no distinct portage here, so you must choose between running the left or right channel. Our group found the one to the right held more water but we had to take it slowly in order to line up properly for the remaining rapids waiting around the corner.

Only ten minutes downstream is Grand Rapids (rated Class I-II), followed by three consecutive Class II drops. Novice paddlers should be warned that the entire section of whitewater is quite extensive and the absence of any clear portages can create absolute mayhem during high water. What's interesting is that the map I purchased from Quebec's canoeing federation does show Grand Rapids having a 550-yard (500 m) portage on the right and the three other rapids with 110-yard (100 m) portages, the first two on the right and the last on the left. But like most other portages marked in the guide, they don't exist.

In our group the experience level was mixed. And since they were my canoes we were using, I was thankful that the water was low enough for us to wade or line down through the worst parts. We still managed to leave quite a bit of canoe paint on the rocks.

Lac Rond, Desert River.

Desert River

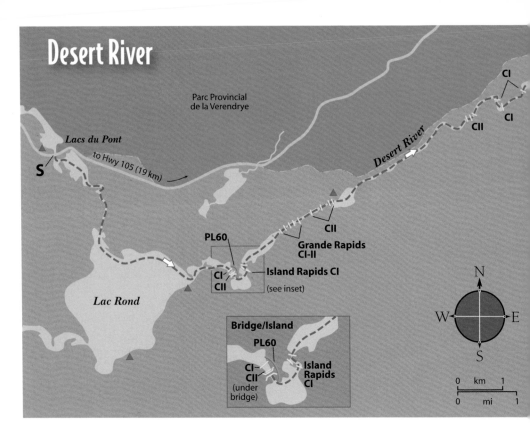

Parc Provincial de la Verendrye

Lacs du Pont

S

to Hwy 105 (19 km)

Desert River

CI

CII

CI

CII

PL60

Grande Rapids CI-II

CII

Island Rapids CI

(see inset)

CI
CII

Lac Rond

Bridge/Island

PL60

CI–CII
(under bridge)

Island Rapids CI

N
W — E
S

0   km   1
0   mi   1

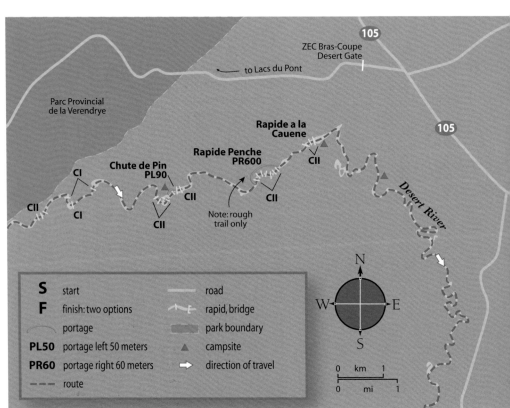

105

ZEC Bras-Coupe Desert Gate

to Lacs du Pont

105

Parc Provincial de la Verendrye

Rapide a la Cauene

CII

Rapide Penche PR600

CI

Chute de Pin PL90

CII

CII

CI

CI

CII

Note: rough trail only

CII

Desert River

S	start		—	road
F	finish: two options			rapid, bridge
	portage			park boundary
PL50	portage left 50 meters		▲	campsite
PR60	portage right 60 meters		⇨	direction of travel
- - -	route			

N
W — E
S

0   km   1
0   mi   1

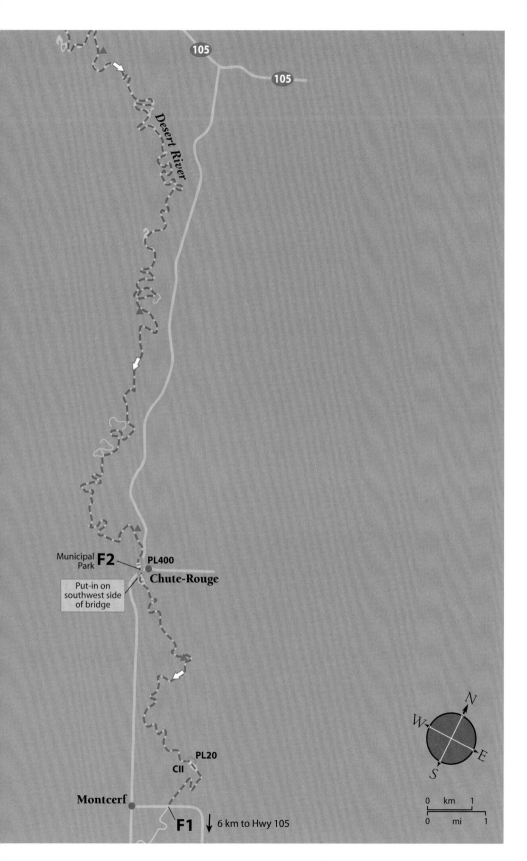

105

105

Desert River

Municipal Park **F2** **PL400**

Chute-Rouge

Put-in on southwest side of bridge

PL20

CII

Montcerf

F1 ↓ 6 km to Hwy 105

N
W   E
S

0   km   1
0   mi   1

Three miles (5 km) downstream from Grand Rapids is another Class II, but it takes about half the time of the last run. Then, just before you reach Chute de Pin, there are three easy Class Is and another set of twin channels to choose from. Our group split up here, with Jeff and Greg heading to the right and Mike and I to the left. Both canoes ground to a halt before reaching the bottom — take note, though, that water levels were at an unusual low.

Chute de Pin is just below the twin channels, where finally, clearly, a 99-yard (90 m) portage avoids the major drop on the left. In keeping with the spirit of the river, however, the portage ends directly below the chute, still leaving you a technical Class II to deal with at the bottom.

Half an hour downstream is Rapide Penche, which came with a faint 660-yard (600 m) portage along the left bank. Of course, we should have realized that any rapid on this river that comes with even a hint of a portage would be extremely technical to run. Blindly we ran it, however, and finished an hour and a half and a roll of duct tape later.

On the Class II that followed (Rapide à la Cauene) we were humble enough to look for a portage, but nothing existed. Our only recourse then was to run, line and wade through the mess of slippery quartzite and foaming whitewater. It wasn't as difficult as Rapid Penche, but we still managed to use up more duct tape.

Soon after Rapide à la Cauene, the river makes a dramatic turn to the right. From here on in, it meanders extensively, the current quite placid for the most part. At almost every bend there's a prime beach campsite. The wooded banks are thick with white birch trees, which is why the Desert River was one of the key harvesting areas for the Algonquin birchbark canoe builders. In fact, strong evidence shows that it was an Algonquin birchbark canoe built around Lac Desert that Samuel de Champlain first saw in 1603 and then adopted for commerce and exploration.

Our group enjoyed an hour of peaceful paddling before choosing one of the sand beaches to make camp on. The site happened to have fresh bear prints on it, but we decided to set the tent up anyway. However, as darkness drew near and I began simmering dinner on the cookstove, we heard a rustle in the back woods. I managed to scare whatever it was off, but a few minutes later we heard the bushes move behind us again. Mike, Greg and Jeff suggested that we leave immediately but dinner was half-cooked and I grew stubborn, clanged some pots and pans together, and the animal ran off once again.

Another half hour passed and everyone began to feel quite settled. Until I began baking brownies, that is. The instant the smell of dessert filled the air, the woods behind us moved again, making the others more determined than ever to break camp and making me more pigheaded about finishing our evening meal in peace. At least, that is, until I caught a glimpse of black fur about 10 yards away. I yelled out, "Hey, bear! Whoa!" The bear reacted by taking a small hop backward, a kind of double-take, and then started heading toward our camp to investigate just whatever had startled it. In seconds we had the canoes loaded and headed downriver to search for another suitable site.

The next day, not wanting to make too many miles too fast, we floated lazily with the current, stopping at almost every beach for a swim and even an extended lunch break at the bottom of one of two Class I rapids we encountered along the way.

About 9 miles (15 km) along, we started seeing signs of civilization — first a herd of cows, then the odd cottage, and finally two naked sunbathers. Then, just as we were feeling comfortable with our slow pace, the banks steepened and funneled the current into a tight channel — Chute-Rouge.

Mike and I hung back from the drop, since we remembered seeing Chute-Rouge during the drive up to the access point. But Jeff and Greg were stuffed into the back of my truck at the time and never did witness what they were now heading for. Luckily, the water was so low that they were able to eddy out before the main chute and then wade back up the first few rapids, humbly joining us at a trail leading up to a roadway on the left. We carried our gear along the road for about 440 yards (400 m), crossed the bridge, and then walked back down to the river by way of a trail found at the end of clearing to the left.

The last 6 miles (10 km) between Chute-Rouge and the take-out at Montcerf has more cottages and cows, and if it weren't for a challenging Class II ledge not long before Montcerf, and the possibility of sighting a few more nude sunbathers, our group would have voted the bridge at Chute-Rouge a better take-out point.

In any case, we made camp at the bottom of the last rapid. There was no real campsite, just a mud flat not even large enough to place a tent on. None of us wanted to end our trip in a cheap hotel in Maniwaki, however. So we unrolled a tarp, dug a pit for the fire and stretched out to watch one of the best displays of northern lights we've ever witnessed. Green lights pulsated across the sky, sometimes sporadic and sometimes with some sense of rhythm. We stayed up well past midnight, pointing out various images formed in the sky (dancing angels, the head of a dragon, a flock of geese, even the phoenix firebird) until the ghostly lights disappeared and the stars were left to light up the sky alone. It was an incredible way to end an incredible journey.

TIME 2 to 3 days

DIFFICULTY Due to the lack of portages around many Class II rapids, canoeists must have at least moderate whitewater experience.

PORTAGES 5

LONGEST PORTAGE
660 yards (600 m)

BEST TIME TO RUN IT The Desert River manages to hold keep its water well, but running it in the spring and fall would save you a lot of wading.

FEE A one- or two-night interior camping permit, as well as a fishing license separate from the regular fishing license, must be purchased at the entrance to Quebec's ZEC Bras-Desert Reserve.

ALTERNATIVE ROUTE The route may be extended all the way to the town of Maniwaki with only Chute à Mercier to portage around, but this may be a monotonous paddle for most.

OUTFITTERS
Martin Canoe & Snowshoe Tours
R.R. 1
960 East County Rd. 50
Harrow, Ontario
N0R 1G0
519-738-3998

FOR MORE INFORMATION
Federation Quebecoise du canot-camping inc.
4545, av. Pierre-De Coubertin
C.P. 1000, Succ. M,
Montreal, Quebec
H1V 3R2
514-252-3001
www.canot-kayak.qc.ca

Association Chasse et Peche de la Desert inc.
69, Principle Nord
Maniwaki, Quebec
J9E 2B5
819-449-3838

MAPS Federation du canot-camping provides a canoe route booklet (in French only).

TOPOGRAPHIC MAPS
31 K/8 & 31 K/9

The Upper Gatineau
Quebec's Playboating Hotspot

I LOOK LIKE A GEEK DRESSED UP AS A PLAYBOATER. But every spring the guys at Wildrock Outfitters in Peterborough somehow persuade me to slip into an embarrassingly tight wetsuit, neoprene booties and a helmet the colors of Neapolitan ice cream and then join them in attempting Stern Squirts, High Rock Boofs, Pirouettes, McTwists, Hairy Ferries and the ultimate Mystery Move — the conversion of a canoe into a submarine, sometimes intentional and sometimes not. Of course, I've yet to master any of these moves. Sometimes I wonder if it's just the greasy hamburgers we order at the local pub when we get back home that really attract me to the sport.

Here's a brief description of one of Wildrock's hotspots — Quebec's Upper Gatineau River. The run has some hazardous Class IV rapids and huge standing waves to contend with, and because the river was still carrying logs up until five years ago, it still holds a number of deadheads and strainers that can become extremely dangerous. So, just be warned, if you don't know the true definition of an Ice-Cream Headache, don't even bother showing up.

From Ottawa take Highway 5, and then Highway 105, north toward Maniwaki. Approximately 12.5 miles (20 km) south of Maniwaki is the small hamlet of Bouchette, where the road crosses the river. This marks the take-out. To begin the trip, however, drive toward where Highway 107 crosses the river, east of Maniwaki,

Sidesurfing L'Anus de Lucifer, Upper Gatineau River.

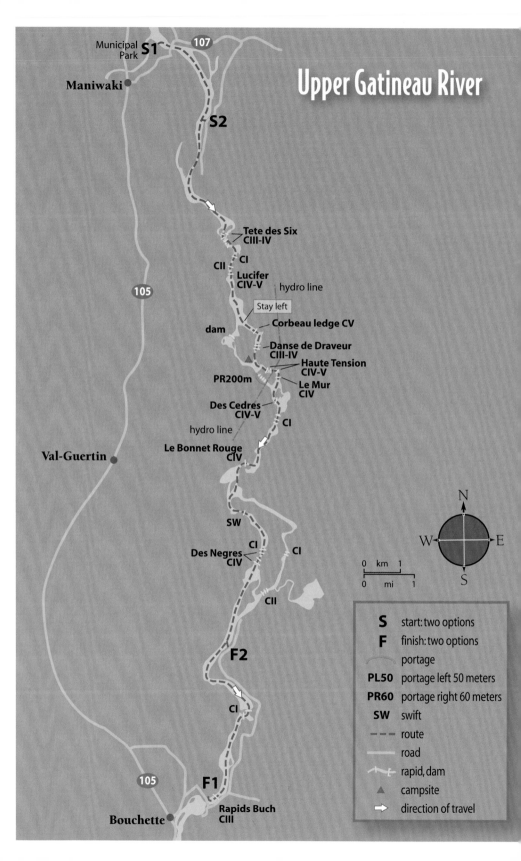

Upper Gatineau River

Municipal Park **S1**

107

Maniwaki

S2

Tete des Six
CIII-IV

CI

CII

Lucifer
CIV-V

hydro line

Stay left

Corbeau ledge CV

dam

Danse de Draveur
CIII-IV

Haute Tension
CIV-V

PR200m

Le Mur
CIV

Des Cedres
CIV-V

CI

hydro line

Le Bonnet Rouge
CIV

Val-Guertin

SW

Des Negres   **CI**
CIV

CI

CII

F2

CI

105

F1

Bouchette

Rapids Buch
CIII

N
W — E
S

| 0 | km | 1 |
| 0 | mi | 1 |

S start: two options
F finish: two options
portage
PL50 portage left 50 meters
PR60 portage right 60 meters
SW swift
--- route
road
rapid, dam
▲ campsite
➤ direction of travel

and either put in at the municipal park on the left or continue along a side road on the southeast side of the river and find a clearing to park your vehicle.

The first rapid comes soon after the put-in. Called Tete des Six (Six Heads), it's made up of numerous Class II and III rapids and a tricky Class V that form between some islands, and is a great place to practice up for the nasty Class IV-V not far downstream. This technical rapid forms three large holes, all of which must be scouted, especially the one on the far right, nicknamed L'Anus de Lucifer (Lucifer's Anus).

Then, down a tight channel to the left, a Class V called Corbeau (The Crow) can be run by taking a narrow passage on center left. Soon after is an easier Class III-IV called Danse de Draveur (Raftman's Dance).

Next, on a second channel to the left, are two more Class IV-V rapids. The first set is directly under some hydro lines — hence the name Haute Tension (High Tension Rapids) — and has some very large standing waves. The second, called Le Mur (The Wall), is just as dangerous, with big holes stuck out in the center; the only safe route is to the extreme right.

What remains are several more technical runs called the Cedars, Red Cap and the Negroes (named after the bodies of two black men were found here at the beginning of the century). All are Class IVs and make for an enjoyable ride all the way down to the take-out.

The Upper Gatineau: Quebec's Playboating Hotspot

TIME 1 day

DIFFICULTY For "extreme" playboaters only!

PORTAGES None — we hope!

BEST TIME TO RUN IT Whenever you think you can handle it!

FEE None

FOR MORE INFORMATION
Madawaska Kanu Camp Inc. /
  Owl Rafting Inc.
Box 29
Foresters Falls, Ontario K0J 1V0
613-646-2307

Wild Rock Outfitters
167 Charlotte Street

Peterborough, Ontario
K9J 2T7
705-745-9133
www.wildrock.net

Federation Quebecoise du canot-camping inc.
4545, av. Pierre-De Coubertin
C.P. 1000, Succ. M
Montreal, Quebec
H1V 3R2
514-252-3001
www.canot-kayak.qc.ca

MAPS Federation Quebecoise de canot-camping has produced a pamphlet (untitled and in French only).

TOPOGRAPHIC MAPS
31 J/4 & 31 J/5

Hugh Banks, showing off a whitefish he caught on the Kinogama River.
Damn! Outfished again.

Bibliography

Armitage, Andrew. *The Sweetwater Explorer: Paddling in Grey and Bruce Counties*. Owen Sound: The Ginger Press, 1995.

Barr, Elinor. *White Otter Castle: The Legacy of Jimmy McQuat*. Thunder Bay, 1984.

Bennet, Doug and Tim Tiner. *Up North: A Guide to Ontario's Wilderness from Blackflies to Northern Lights*. Reed Books Canada, 1993.

Buckley, Beth and Dave. "Paddling Algoma's Sand River." Kanawa, spring 1996.

Campbell, William A. *The French and Pickerel Rivers, Their History and Their People*. Sudbury, Ont.: Journal Printing, 1986.

Coombe, Geraldine. *Muskoka Past and Present*. Toronto; New York: McGraw-Hill Ryerson, 1976.

Dewdney, Selwyn and Kenneth E. Kidd. *Indian Rock Paintings of the Great Lakes*. Toronto: University of Toronto Press, 1973.

Dickson, James. *Camping in the Muskoka Region: A Story of Algonquin Park*. Toronto: Ontario Department of Lands and Forests, 1960.

Federation Quebecoise du canot-camping inc. Riviere Desert pamphlet. 1997.

——. Riviere Garineau pamphlet. 1997.

——. Riviere Coulonge booklet. 1998 edition.

——. Riviere Dumoine booklet. 1993 edition.

——. Carte 6 - Reserve Faunique La Verendrye map. 1996.

Friends of Algonquin Park. *Canoe Routes of Algonquin Park*. 1996.

Friends of Algonquin Park. *Whiskey Rapids Trail: Algonquin River Ecology*. 1992.

Friends of the Mattawa River *Heritage Park. Mattawa River Heritage Map*. 1997.

Friends of White Otter Castle. *Souvenir Booklet of the White Otter Castle 1992-1994*. 1996.

Gage, S. R. *A Few Rustic Huts: Ranger Cabins and Logging Camp Buildings of Algonquin Park*. Oakville: Mosiac Press, 1985.

Garland, G. D. *Glimpses of Algonquin: Thirty Personal Impressions from Earliest Times to the Present*. Whitney: Friends of Algonquin Park, 1994.

Gidmark, David. *Birchbark Canoe: Living Among the Algonquin*. Willowdale, Ont.: Firefly Books, 1997.

Hargreaves, Jim. *Ottawa River Whitewater: A Paddler's Guide to the Middle and Main Channels*. Hargreaves, 1998.

Harting, Tony. *French River: Canoeing the River of the Stick-Wavers*. Erin: Boston Mills Press, 1996.

Henderson, Bob. "The White Otter Castle." Kanawa, spring 1998.

Hodgins, Bruce W. and Jamie Benidickson. *The Temagami Experience: Recreation, Resource, and Aboriginal Rights in the Northern Ontario Wilderness*. Toronto: University of Toronto Press, 1989.

Holley, Frank. *Just Passing Through: The People and the Places North of Matachewan*. Cobolt: The Highway Book Shop, 1988.

http://www. sepaq.com/pages/reser80a.html

http://www.webpan.com/canoeroutes/Route...Ontario/Northeast/pishkanogami/route.htm

Legget, Robert Ferguson. *Rideau Waterway*. Toronto: University of Toronto Press, 1986.

Long, Gary. *This River The Muskoka*. Erin: The Boston Mills Press, 1989.

Mackay, Roderick. *Spirits of the Little Bonnechere: A History of Exploration and Settlement 1800 to 1920*. Pembroke: Friends of Bonnechere Park, 1996.

Ministry of Natural Resources, Chapleau District. Pishkanogami Canoe Route pamphlet. 1984.

———. Mississagi River Canoe Route pamphlet. 1976.

Ministry of Natural Resources, Ignace District. Turtle River Provincial Park Canoe Route map. 1996.

Ministry of Natural Resources, Ignace District. Turtle River Provincial Waterway Park Background Information. 1990.

Ministry of Natural Resources, Lake Superior Provincial Park. Canoeing in Lake Superior Provincial Park pamphlet. 1990.

Ministry of Natural Resources, North Bay District. Restoule–Upper French Canoe Route pamphlet. 1984.

Ministry of Natural Resources, Parks and Recreational Areas Branch, in cooperation with McClelland and Stewart. Canoe Routes of Ontario. Toronto: 1981.

Ministry of Natural Resources, Sudbury District. French River Canoe Map. 1994.

Ministry of Natural Resources, Swastika District. Gowganda to Matachewan Canoe Route pamphlet. 1984.

Ministry of Natural Resources, Temagami District. Canoeing in the Temagami Area (map). Temagami, Ont.

Passfield, Robert W. *Building The Rideau Canal: A Pictorial History*. Don Mills Ontario: Fitzhenry & Whiteside in association with Parks Canada, 1982.

Reid, Ron and Janet Grand. *Canoeing Ontario's Rivers*. Vancouver/Toronto: Douglas & McIntyre, 1985.

Runtz, Michael. *The Explorer's Guide to Algonquin Park*. Erin: The Boston Mills Press, 1993.

Saugeen Country Tourism Association. Saugeen River Canoe Route pamphlet. 1998.

Sloan, Tony A. *Blackflies and White Water*. McClelland and Stewart Limited, 1977.

Turner, Larry. *Rideau*. Toronto: Boston Mills Press, 1995.

Wilson, Hap. *Rivers of the Upper Ottawa Valley: Myth, Magic and Adventure*. With the Canadian Recreational Canoe Association, 1993.

———. *Riviere Dumoine: A Comprehensive Guide for the Adventuring Canoeist*. With the Canadian Recreational Canoe Association, 1987.

For information about the Canadian Recreational Canoeing Association and to find out how to subscribe to *KANAWA, Canada's Canoeing and Kayaking Magazine*, contact the Canadian Recreational Canoeing Association, Box 398, 446 Main Street West, Merrickville, Ontario, K0G 1N0. You can also reach them at 1-888-252-6292 (toll free), 613-269-2910 (phone), and 613-269-2908 (fax). Visit the CRCA website at www.paddlingcanada.com.